The Tragicomedy
of **Public Education**

Laughing
and
Crying
Thinking
and
Fixing

JAMES M. KAUFFMAN

P.O. Box 930160
Verona, Wisconsin 53593-0160 USA
Phone 1-800-327-4269   Fax 1.800.942.3865

www.AttainmentCompany.com

Author: James M. Kauffman, University of Virginia
Editor: Tom Kinney

ISBN 1-57861-682-4

Dedication

This book is dedicated to the students in our public schools, all of whom deserve an education that is neither tragic nor comic but simply the best education we can give them.

Contents

Preface

My central message is that we've got to make public education a lot better, but that we can't really do that until we understand how and why it's so screwed up. First, we need to laugh about things that may make us want to cry. Then we need to think carefully about education and get serious about making our schools better.

One reason public education is in such a mess is that too many people have cried about how bad it is and then tried to fix it without thinking much about it. This is about as smart as observing that your car isn't running right, then getting mad and hitting it with a hammer. If you did this, you'd look foolish and make a lot of people laugh. You'd be comedic without intending to be, just like people who want to fix education because they're mad about schools and don't know what to do except say something cockeyed.

People who should know better have said things about education that are wildly off base yet funny. In doing so, they've made public education in America a tragicomedy. They obviously haven't thought very much about education; they are just blathering. Their nonsense does nothing to make education better. It makes a mockery of the idea that we want to teach children to be critical thinkers. Makes me want to cry and scream! But laughing about it first is better than crying and screaming. If you don't see what's funny, your crying isn't going to help. Screaming doesn't help either. And if you don't figure out what's tragicomic about public education, then you won't know what to do to fix the problem.

I'm sure you have the good sense to ask why anyone should take my comments seriously—or even laugh as I suggest. So, I'll tell you something about my experience and my views. I've been a classroom teacher at the elementary and middle school levels in both special and general education. Beginning in 1970, I taught students who were preparing to become special education teachers, and I also worked with advanced graduate students in education at the University of Virginia. Education has been my professional life since 1962 (for more about me, you can go to www.people.virginia.edu/~jmk9t/ and see what I've been up to professionally since the early 1960s). Most of my time has been spent in educating exceptional children and studying special education.

I think that what I've written is sensible and trustworthy, but you should consider very carefully whom and what to trust, because public education has in many ways become the dumping ground of bad, scientifically unverified programming, worse ideas, and poor thinking about education in general. The fact that I've been an educator for a long time doesn't mean that I know what I'm talking about; some people with long experience in a given field of work may misunderstand it and say very silly things about it. The fact that I have an advanced degree doesn't mean that what I say or write makes sense; some people with lots of formal education sometimes say or write things that someone with far less schooling can see is claptrap. The fact that I've written a lot about special education doesn't mean that what I write is on the money; lots of gibberish gets published. Read with your brain fully engaged. That's what we expect of kids in school. We should expect it of ourselves.

I've come to realize that most people don't think a lot about public education, much less special education. They aren't expected to, and they don't have to. Why should they? It's only people like me, who've devoted their working lives to education, who *have* to think about it very much. And even some of *us* slip a cog now and then. We just need to recognize when cogs are slipping, whether we're special or general educators or neither.

Those who don't have to think much about education can be excused for thinking poorly about it. After all, even reasonably bright people when asked to think about things they haven't much thought about (like my thinking about astrophysics) often botch the job. They might get caught up in poor reasoning since they don't have the basic information they need, or because they forget critical pieces of information, or simply because they ignore basic facts apparent to those who are knowledgeable about the field. Still, every field of study has its crackpots and embarrassingly incompetent thinkers. Unfortunately, some people who've spent a lot of time as educators don't think productively about their business either. We need to laugh at their nonsense.

So we have this problem of some people who are intelligent but uninvolved in education, and some who are both intelligent and experienced educators doing some very poor thinking about education, especially the education of atypical children. A person can be a good thinker about one thing but not another, or be a good thinker sometimes and at other times not. Good and bad thinking aren't always on or always off, so we have to be careful not to conclude that a person who's brilliant sometimes or at some things is *always* brilliant or that a person whose thinking *sometimes* goes haywire is unintelligent.

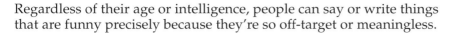

Regardless of their age or intelligence, people can say or write things that are funny precisely because they're so off-target or meaningless.

I must admit that some of the things I've read and heard about both special and general education in the past half century or so have been very amusing to me. And I'm guessing that a lot of what you've read is amusing to you, too. In fact, my assumption is that we'd agree that much of this errant thinking would be *only* comical if the consequences of its being taken seriously weren't so tragic for the kids, parents, and teachers involved, not to mention our society. For those of us who take public education seriously and see the damage done by poor thinking about it, it's tragicomic—laughable, yet with horrifying implications.

A lot of my comments are aimed at special education and the parents of exceptional children. Note, however, that special education and general education are no longer separate educational entities. Special education is now an integral part of general education in the public schools, and more and more exceptional children—those with disabilities and those with special gifts and talents and those with both—are being taught in general classrooms. That is, teachers with little or no training in special education are being given responsibility for teaching exceptional children, and students with special educational needs are increasingly being placed in the same schools and classrooms they would attend if they were typical students. Thus, what happens to education in the general case—how people think, what and how they think children should be taught, the policies they make—is something about which all of us should be concerned. Special education is increasingly integrated into general education, and parents would be foolish, indeed, to do either of the following: ignore general education or assume that special education doesn't concern their children.

About the organization of this book

This little book has two sections. In Part I, I describe how too much of what is said and thought about public education is simultaneously tragic and comic. I also explain how people have used poor thinking to hoodwink others. Then I look at the awful consequences of foolishness taken seriously—the tragic results of letting ourselves be fooled by nonsense. In Part II, I suggest how we might think better about public education. I outline the steps we should take to make better sense of educational problems and make rational proposals for change.

Certainly, this book doesn't say it all. There's a lot more to say about education, but I hope this at least puts many readers on the road to

recognizing ludicrous statements about schools and schooling when they read or hear them. I hope some of the quotes I use and some of the comments I offer make readers laugh. I hope reading the book also puts them on the road to insisting that all of us—the general public, educators, and policy makers alike—talk and write more sensibly about one of the most important aspects of public life in a democracy, its public education system.

I'm grateful to more people than I can name for their support in writing this little book. My dear wife, Patty Pullen, is extraordinarily talented at working with people, including children, and writing about her experiences. She's a former teacher extraordinaire, and it's no wonder I wanted her as a life partner in every conceivable way. She patiently read and reread the manuscript and gave me the feedback of an insightful and skillful special education teacher, parent, and writer whose work is always fun to read. My confidence was greatly increased by the comments and suggestions of Barbara Bateman, a wise, thoughtful, and caring lawyer, teacher, special education researcher, and writer whose work I've admired for more than four decades. She writes and speaks with exceptional clarity, and her praise and encouragement have been invaluable. And I must credit her with suggesting the book's subtitle: *Laughing and Crying, Thinking and Fixing*. My friend Sarah Irvine, another writer and editor of great talent, read parts of an early draft of the manuscript and gave me support and useful comments. Finally, I am particularly grateful to Tom Kinney, my editor at Full Court Press, for his faith in my work, his insightful and gentle guidance, and his invaluable help in saying things with greater clarity and force.

JMK

Charlottesville, VA

Author

James M. Kauffman

James M. Kauffman is Professor Emeritus of Education at the University of Virginia, where he has been chair of the Department of Special Education, Associate Dean for Research, the Charles S. Robb Professor of Education, and the William Clay Parrish, Jr. Professor of Education. He is a former teacher in both general elementary and special education for students with emotional and behavioral disorders.

Kauffman received his Ed.D. in special education from the University of Kansas in 1969. He is a past president of the Council for Children with Behavioral Disorders (CCBD), and among his honors are the 2002 Outstanding Leadership Award from CCBD and the 1994 Research Award of the Council for Exceptional Children. He served as director of doctoral study in special education at the University of Virginia and taught seminars in special education.

He is author or coauthor of numerous publications in special education, including the following books: *Exceptional Learners: Introduction to Special Education* (11th ed., 2009), *Characteristics of Emotional and Behavioral Disorders of Children and Youth* (9th ed., 2009), *Learning Disabilities: Foundations, Characteristics, and Effective Teaching* (3rd ed., 2005), *Special Education: What It Is and Why We Need It* (2005), *The Illusion of Full Inclusion: A Comprehensive Critique of a Current Special Education Bandwagon* (2nd ed., 2005), *Children and Youth with Emotional and Behavioral Disorders: A History of Their Education* (2006), and *Classroom Behavior Management: A Reflective Case-Based Approach* (5th ed. in press, 2011).

For more information, see Kauffman's website at www.people.virginia.edu/~jmk9t/.

Part I
Laughing and Crying

Containing six expository chapters on:

1. How education needs improvement but is made worse by tragicomic suggestions

2. How education becomes tragicomic when truth is displaced by truthiness

3. How the art of poor thinking is practiced with tragicomic effects on education

4. How slogans and trite phrases sabotage common sense and contribute to the tragicomedy of education

5. How poor thinking drove us off track, creating a tragicomic train wreck of ideas

6. How the tragicomic consequences of poor thinking about education waste time and money and hurt children

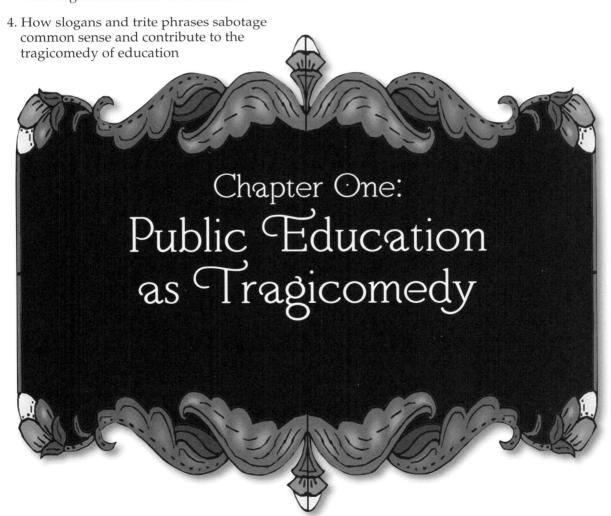

Chapter One:
Public Education as Tragicomedy

How Education Needs Improvement but Is Made Worse by Tragicomic Suggestions

Children are no joke. Unfortunately, their education too often is. But their education doesn't have to be miserable. We can make public education better, even make it what it should be. But to do so, we need to see more clearly that much of what's said about it and the policies that govern it are silly and off target and then get serious about its improvement. It's healthy for us to see the comic as well as the tragic in public schooling. In fact, seeing the comic side of children's education is essential. My advice is this: laugh before you cry. *See the absurd, the funny, the ridiculous in what people say and apparently think, and laugh at it before you cry.*

Laugh and cry, but then think things through and take action to make the education of children better. You must take action, and in later chapters I will suggest some things you can do about your own thinking and advocacy with policy makers. Laughing is good for you. It's also the most effective weapon, and sometimes our only weapon, against injustice. And there's injustice aplenty to laugh and cry about in the education of all children, including exceptional children. *But laugh first.*

General and special education: both tragicomic

Most children receive general education—which is intended for typical children. We assume that general education is appropriate for the students it serves, but often it isn't. Too often it isn't really good for any child, which is maddening and shameful. We need to make it better, so that it better serves the needs of children and society.

Special education is designed for students who are atypical—not like most in ways that are important for their education. Exceptional children need a different, special education. By definition, their educational needs are not those of the typical child. The tragicomedy of their miseducation is a national disgrace and a professional embarrassment. Our children with special needs deserve better. Their education must be taken seriously and made what it should be— teaching that makes maximum use of their abilities and will help them acquire the skills they need to prosper to the full extent that they can as adults.

Special education is mentioned often in this book. This is because more children with exceptionalities—either disabilities or special gifts and talents or both—are being educated in the mainstream of public education. They're "included" in general education for a significant part of their time in school. Therefore, I can't focus *solely* on either general or special education. Special education has to be seen in the context of general education—as something that often occurs in neighborhood schools and in classrooms where most children are taught.

Too many general education teachers give little or no acknowledgment to special education or to the exceptional children it's designed to serve. Their assumption seems to be that all children are special, so none of their students really has a special (significantly different instructional) need. For example, award-winning general education teacher Rafe Esquith makes no mention whatsoever of special education or students with disabilities in his popular book, *Teach Like Your Hair's on Fire*.[1] I suppose you could assume that if the teacher teaches well, then children with disabilities are just like everyone else in the class, so no one needs to mention them. Or you might assume that some teachers don't recognize exceptional children when they see them. They might recognize them and just choose to ignore them. Probably the assumption that exceptional children are often unrecognized or ignored in general education is safer. Treating exceptional children just like all the other students might help teachers and administrators, and it might even help some exceptional children, but it won't help them all. And the very idea that general and special education aren't really different is laughable.

We get the joke when someone says, "I'm special, just like everyone else." That kind of nonsense at least makes us smile, if not laugh. Why don't we get the joke and laugh people out of leadership positions when they say that *all* children should be getting special education? We shouldn't take nonsense seriously, yet we too often do when people intone nonsense about education. Why don't we laugh at politicians who demand that every child become proficient in reading when that is simply not feasible? We too often let such craven pandering go, or respond as if it's a serious proposal.

Comedians' use of tragicomedy

Our most endearing comics and social critics have often used tragic events or absurdities as the basic material for their commentaries that make us laugh. They've understood that we should laugh at absurdity regardless of who or what created it—regardless of religion, creed, social standing, or personal characteristic, even if it's our own. They get the comic side of tragedy; it's in their job description. Often they make us want to laugh and cry at the same time. Special and general education are both like that—absurd and silly but pitiful and heartbreaking, too.

Mark Twain understood tragicomedy, perhaps more keenly than all but a few. Having grown up in Hannibal, Missouri, his boyhood town, I have an unusual affection for his humor, which was frequently directed at the everyday lunacies of the social order. Many people know that he said, "Clothes make the man." Few know the rest of the quote: "Naked people have little or no influence in society."[2]

Mark Twain made us laugh at the funny side of social injustice, absurd statements, natural catastrophes, and personal failings. He saw tragicomedy where others saw only tragedy or comedy. A topic might be serious, but that didn't stop him from poking fun. He might say something in jest, but that didn't mean the underlying issue wasn't serious. He understood that laughter is the only really effective weapon we have when it comes to the mess people make of things. Consider his send-up of the pompous yet dense and ultimately inane language of nineteenth-century medical science in his story "Those Extraordinary Twins":

> Without going too much into detail, madam—for you would probably not understand it anyway—I concede that great care is going to be necessary here; otherwise exudation of the oesophagus is nearly sure to ensue, and this will be followed by ossification and extradition of the maxillaris superioris, which must decompose the granular surfaces of the great infusorial ganglionic system, thus obstructing the action of the posterior varioloid arteries, and precipitating compound strangulated sorosis of the valvular tissues, and ending unavoidably in the dispersion and combustion of the marsupial fluxes and the consequent embrocation of the bicuspid populo redax referendum rotulorum.[3]

Mark Twain saw the humor in such language, which was intended to be unintelligible. We realize that he throws real words together with neologisms (made up words) to provide a pastiche of knowledge (a jumble of words that imitates a style but reflects silliness rather than knowledge). His ability to make us laugh in the face of a serious problem is part of the charm and humor of the story. He had great fun with incomprehensibility, regardless of its source. Laughter is, after all, the response we should have to things that don't make sense, whether they're found in medicine, religion, politics, or education.

Twain made fun of all religions, and his comments about Christian Science are typical. He noted that the basic tenets of the religion are, in his words, "strange . . . frantic, and incomprehensible" and that in the book describing it (*Divine Science*) often "the words do not seem to have any traceable meaning." He noted also that many people claim to understand it and claim "that there [are] no such things as pain, sickness and death, and no realities in the world; nothing actually existent but Mind." He concluded his check-up of Christian Science by dryly noting, "[This] seems to me to modify the value of their testimony."[4]

In the 1860s, Twain wrote in letters from Hawaii, "I have seen a number of legislatures, and there was a comfortable majority in each of them that knew just about enough to come in when it rained, and that was all."[5] He recorded the fact that one Hawaiian legislator suggested building a suspension bridge from Oahu to Hawaii, a distance of about 150 miles over open ocean. This legislator made his proposal in all seriousness, not intending to be funny, while ignoring the engineering realities. He was funny without intending to be, and Twain didn't let him get away with it unscathed. Twain also observed that in the Wisconsin legislature of the era, "a member got up and seriously suggested that when a man committed the damning crime of arson they ought either to hang him or make him marry the girl!" Twain concluded in his inimitable style, "To my mind the suspension-bridge man was a Solomon compared to this idiot."[6]

Too bad that Mark Twain's mind is gone from this world. At least his wit has been preserved in writing. But we admire him for more than his wit. He also had a more finely tuned sense of social justice than most of his contemporaries, including a sense of shame about slavery and racial discrimination. Roy Blount, Jr., quoted Mark Twain's observation that "The skin of every human being contains a slave," adding his own comment: "He could at least make America flinch before it laughed."[7]

In our own era, Garrison Keillor understands the humor in absurdity. With his radio show, *A Prairie Home Companion*, he makes us smile, if

not laugh aloud, at preposterous commercials for things like biscuits and catsup and duct tape and at the absurd ideas that in the mythical Lake Wobegon (or in any real town) *all* of the women can be strong, *all* of the men can be good looking, and *all* of the children can be above average. In Lake Wobegon, we can also assume that all children are very, very "special."

A tragicomic education

Which brings me back to the topic of this book—the tragicomedy of special and general education. In some ways, the story of education in the United States is inspiring. In other ways it's tragic, almost beyond belief. The tragic aspects of special and general education make a lot of people who really care about it want to cry, and they make no one happy. While they also have their comic aspects, it's the kind of dark humor about which you laugh to keep from crying. It's good for us to laugh at some of the more obvious mistakes and the silliness of the sad story that education has become, because the alternatives—tears or rage—are less satisfying.

We love our schools; we hate what's happening to them. "We" includes people regardless of ethnic origins, color, or gender. It includes students with disabilities and their families. It includes typical students and their families and gifted students and theirs. It includes the political left and right. We're all in this together—all concerned about education's improvement, its fairness, its future. We need to laugh and cry with each other because our collective futures are at stake.

The tragedy is that we don't have the schools we want and need. Adults need better schools to prepare students for productive lives. Children need better schools to make their lives happier and their futures brighter. The heartbreak of schools is that they're so often not what they should be. The comedy is that people so often make absurd analyses of educational problems and propose cockeyed solutions to these problems. Poor thinking about education, special and general, and schools, neighborhood and special, too often results in high comedy.

If we care about our schools and education, then we must think about how to make them what we want them to be. And in thinking about this, we need to understand why education is tragicomic—why, in the middle of all the care and concern people have about educating children, we have to be able to see the ridiculous for what it is, to see the comical side of the tragedy.

We may laugh about education, whether special or general, but we also want very much to avoid adding to its tragic features. Thank goodness we can avoid making things worse if we're willing to look at education with renewed emphasis on clear and careful thinking and if we're able to see the comedy in the tragically flawed statements and proposals that educators, government officials, business leaders, journalists, and others make about education. Remember Twain's send-up of pompous, unintelligible language? Imagine his reaction to the following commentary from an education professional's book. It's as silly as Twain's fictional nineteenth-century physician's advice to Aunt Polly, and it's longer!

> The reduction of possible interpretations to the demands of "basic language" or the increased surveillance of unauthorized interpretations through the imposition of a metalanguage create [sic] definitively favorable conditions for "consensus." In other words, once we learn the right use of language (as put forth through the performativity principle of capitalist technoscience or a universal normativity), the "true" meaning behind the proliferation of second-order meanings will shine forth. With only "correct" meanings in circulation, consensus would be "natural.". . . In order for the discussion to go further, to take different directions, to open it up to "the event," dissensus or paralogy must be introduced. However, within the domain of performativity (which both "basic language" and metaprescriptive norms enforce), paralogy would be reduced to mere innovation of contents within the ordained form. If paralogy is understood as the invention of new, imaginative moves not prescripted by the norms, then paralogy is directed at the forms themselves. The intent of paralogy is the creation of new idioms (forms and expressions) for thought. Paralogical moves ensure that any metanarratives do not terminally congeal into totalitarian imperatives . . .[8]

Regardless of the author's intention, this kind of pomposity is funny. So are illogic and unintelligibility. All of these—pomposity, illogic, and unintelligibility—can also be tragic, but only if they're taken seriously. Unfortunately, these kinds of discussions are taken seriously by educators. Too few poke fun at them or see the humor in silly statements about serious things.

Take note that the tragicomedy of the following quotation is amplified by its presence in an official journal of the American Educational Research Association. Note also that, like Twain's story about the nineteenth-century physician, this brimming nonsense that follows,

that seems to go on forever, is but a single sentence. It's funny in its own way, but unfortunately it wasn't *intended* to be funny, like Mark Twain's fictional physician's mumbo jumbo.

> Because of the cultural studies [sic] emphases on working on the cutting edge of theory and theorizing; taking the popular seriously; doing not only interdisciplinary but anti-disciplinary and even post-disciplinary work; undertaking praxis rather than theory or practice, and so forth, we are likely to see (indeed we are already seeing) a greater emphasis on curriculum theorizing that employs cutting edge theory and juxtaposes a number of theoretical discourses; deals with popular culture, the new media (taking up television and the World Wide Web rather differently than current dominant approaches), and a very expanded notion of pedagogy and pedagogical spaces; and utilizes an inter/anti/post-disciplinary approach.[9]

But, if this doesn't tickle your funny bone, try any of many other articles published by the American Educational Research Association,[10] including this gem: "To this end, I believe that our responsibility is to keep educational research in play, increasingly unintelligible to itself, in order to produce different knowledge and produce knowledge differently as we work for social justice in the human sciences."[11] When I read such things as the examples I've given from the literature on education by educators, I can't help recalling Twain's pithy aside: "(It is very curious, the effect which Christian Science has upon the verbal bowels. Particularly the Third Degree; it makes one think of a dictionary with the cholera. But I only thought this; I did not say it.)"[12]

Tragicomic statements of noneducators

Unfortunately, the tragicomedy isn't just a matter of what educators say and write about education. This hyper-gibberish has escaped the campus and is spreading virally into the public sector. Remember what Mark Twain said about the legislator who misunderstood (or, at least, misused) the word "arson"? Twain wasn't particularly kind in his comments about that guy, but his description made us laugh by pointing out the absurdity of the legislator's misunderstanding. Consider the misuse of the word "elite" in the following statement by a group of business leaders. With italics used to emphasize its nonsense, the writers at the National Center on Education and the Economy said, "The challenge is to provide *an elite education for everyone*."[13]

I read this and said to myself, "Whoa, Nelly!" Did these people mean to use hyperbole to make a point? After all, what does "elite" mean?

I think it refers to a small group of people who have more of something (like power or social standing or wealth) than most. It indicates high rank, a hierarchy, which in turn implies there are lower ranks. Everyone being high-ranked is as illogical as everyone being above average or "special." I think these business leaders could've said "better" or "good" or "acceptable" or "decent" and it would make sense. We know that hyperbole is used in fairy tales and in sales pitches and other things that aren't quite real. But, really, "elite for everyone?" Trust me, we're adults; we're ready for real-world statements about education, whether special or general, not things written for children or commercials. If business leaders want the public to believe that if everyone buys their product then everyone will be elite, that's fine. That's business. Education isn't exactly a business, and it isn't improved by commercial slogans. In fact, the call for an elite education for everyone isn't just preposterous. It's certain to fail because it's— well, just impossible!

Or think about the plain meaning of the word "behind" and its misuse in the George W. Bush administration's signature legislation, the No Child Left Behind Act (NCLB). Ordinarily, "left behind" might be taken as a figure of speech, meaning forgotten or neglected. But it's clear from the legislation itself that that's not what it means. It refers to test scores and an expectation of universal proficiency, the kind of test score comparisons that are absurd and that demand we take "left behind" literally, not figuratively. In the context of test scores—something I take up in later chapters—"behind" means someone else is in front or ahead. It doesn't mean forgotten. It doesn't mean neglected. It implies an order, like 1, 2, 3, or first, second, third. G. W. Bush's first secretary of education (well, yes, an educator) stated, "If I'm honored to be confirmed by the Senate, I will dedicate myself every day to the task of assuring that no child in America will be left behind."[14] Twain would have had fun with this. Keillor could have. We should.

And we should understand this: Regardless of who supports the Lake Wobegon-like ideas of NCLB, they are deserving of ridicule. The outright silliness of NCLB is not a matter of political affiliation, as it received strong bipartisan support. NCLB may well be replaced by another equally absurd law under a different name, but if its assumptions about testing are not changed, it will still be ridiculous. More on this later. President Barack Obama's secretary of education, Arnie Duncan, "said he will not back away from testing and accountability,"[15] but if he doesn't back away from universal

proficiency and other absurd ideas in what is now NCLB, he will have fallen into the same irrationality as his predecessors. Irrationality isn't peculiar to a political party.

We should start by laughing at silly uses of words that can't mean what they say, titles or slogans or combinations of words or statements reflecting ludicrous thinking. Here's why. Laughing at something funny is an appropriate first response. However, some funny events also have dangerous consequences, and besides laughing we need to respond to them. Too often we neither laugh nor take appropriate action. We then fail in two ways: first, by not laughing at funny things; second, by not trying to stop something dangerous. Our failure even to laugh demonstrates our willingness to ignore reality.

Why the tragicomedy?

A reasonable question is, "Why do people say things about special or general education that are nonsensical?" Perhaps they believe what they say sounds good or is likely to get them votes or public approval, and nobody will think carefully about what they've said. As Nicholas Lemann wrote in *The New Yorker* about President Bush's education policy initiatives, "The whole world will not be watching. The whole world will be too confused to follow the action."[16] If no one understands, no one will get too upset about the consequences of talking fantasy about real-world issues. What someone says may be the stuff of high comedy, but the tragedy is that many don't recognize it as such. They take nonsense about education seriously.

Too often, any statement about education or its reform goes unchallenged, regardless of how funny or off base it is in its failure to conform to the real world. Consequently, the improvement of education remains stymied while we pursue imaginary solutions. As a society we've not only allowed but supported and sometimes even enshrined in law preposterous propositions about education. Silly talk and pretense have too often been allowed to dominate talk about education. This produces babble, not constructive conversation. It contributes to the tragicomedy of public education.

One misguided response is the suggestion that the language people use is trivial if their *intention*—what they're really after—is honorable. So, the argument goes, we shouldn't pick on the language of the No Child Left Behind policy because, actually, its intention is to improve education, general and special. But, as George Orwell pointed out in the middle of the twentieth century, our language reveals much

about how we think about things, and our thinking is reflected in our language. He wrote:

> But an effect can become a cause, reinforcing the original cause and producing the same effect in an intensified form, and so on indefinitely. A man may take a drink because he feels himself to be a failure, and then fail all the more completely because he drinks. It is rather the same thing that is happening to the English language. It becomes ugly and inaccurate because our thoughts are foolish, but the slovenliness of our language makes it easier for us to have foolish thoughts. The point is that the process is reversible.[17]

The Orwell quotation says to us that a careful analysis of language reveals a great deal about how people think. In fact, we know a lot about what people think by listening carefully to what they say or paying careful attention to what they write. He also described how language is used for political purposes and wrote, "if thought corrupts language, language can also corrupt thought."[18] But mumbo jumbo is used not just in politics and education. Dense, confusing language is sometimes used to fool stockholders in business reports when companies are doing poorly.[19] We're in dangerous territory, indeed, if we assume that what people say has little relationship to what they think and vice versa. But Orwell's last sentence also gives us hope. It says that what we say and think about education can be made better—certainly more accurate, perhaps less ugly as well. We could start by doing what comes naturally when we see an absurdity—laughing about it.

The consequences of silly words

We may conclude that when people use words that don't make sense, or words that have to be redefined to make sense, or use language that's impenetrable, unnecessarily confusing, or otherwise misleading about the true nature of their intention, an event, or a condition, then they are either clueless or up to no good. Writing that can't be deciphered logically or that isn't simple and straightforward isn't helpful. Writers and speakers who can't be easily understood, especially when their topic is the everyday world, probably have either nothing worthwhile to say or, worse, something to hide. We need clearer, less confusing, simpler, more interpretable, and more accurate language in communication about education. When our language and our thinking about it become clearer and more rational, education will become less a tragicomedy and more of what we want it to be.

Nobody who knows schools, teachers, and education believes that things are perfect the way they are. And no one, as far as I know, suggests this. Some people see our schools as catastrophic failures, while others think they're doing a pretty good job, all things considered. The truth is probably somewhere between the most positive and negative appraisals. Our schools certainly aren't total failures, but they need a lot more improvement than the most optimistic views of them suggest. And special education, in particular, needs a lot of improvement. Language that's detached from reality doesn't help us improve schools or education. What's tragic is that people can say comical things about education, whether it's general or special, but not be met with guffaws or, at least, chuckles.

We can and must do better

Education isn't a hopeless case. We can have happier days in both special and general education, days in which things make sense, kids learn more, kids are happier, and we waste less money and time. But having happier days requires changes in the way we talk, think, and act. We have to be more realistic about what education is, what can and can't be done. We have to be able to distinguish fantasy from reality, bad language from language that communicates effectively, good thinking from poor, justifiable conclusions from those that aren't trustworthy.

But our *first* response to absurdity, regardless of its source or its topic, should be bemusement—seeing the laughable in spite of the tragedy. After we have a good laugh, crying is okay. But, ultimately, we must think better and figure out how to fix things.

Notes for Chapter One

[1] Esquith (2007)

[2] Mark Twain Foundation (1976, p. 942)

[3] Twain (1894/1969, p. 288)

[4] Clemens (1899 [1976], p. 383)

[5] Day (1966, p. 109)

[6] Day (1966, p. 112)

[7] Blount (2001, p. 81)

[8] Bain (1995, pp. 7–8)

[9] Wright (2000, p. 7)

[10] See, for example, Erickson & Gutierrez (2002), Pillow (2000),
and St. Pierre (2000)

[11] St. Pierre (2000, p. 27)

[12] Clemens (1899 [1976], p. 378)

[13] National Center on Education and the Economy (1989, p. 9, italics
in original)

[14] Slevin (2000, p. A6)

[15] Glod (2009, p. A2)

[16] Lemann (2001, p. 34)

[17] Orwell (1954, p. 163)

[18] Orwell (1954, p. 174)

[19] Tong (2006)

Part I
Laughing and Crying

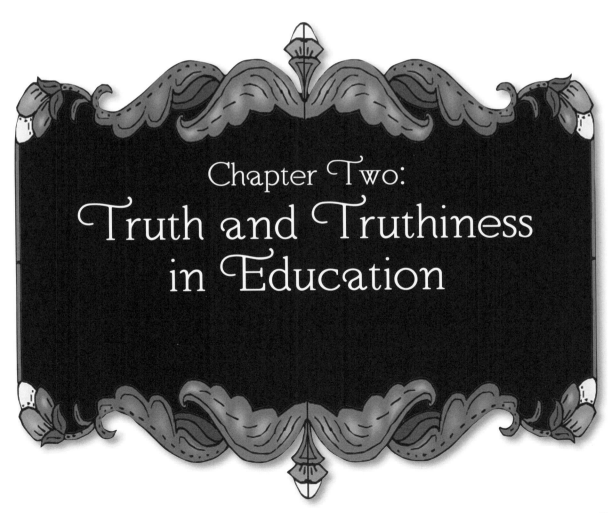

Chapter Two:
Truth and Truthiness in Education

How Education Becomes Tragicomic When Truth Is Displaced by Truthiness

Yes, a lot of what's been said about public education brings us both laughter and tears. But wait until you read about truth vs. truthiness. Then you'll have an additional reason to laugh, and cry, because there are people who in all seriousness believe there is no actual truth. Truth, to them, is just sort of truthy-ish. Yet they're dead serious. Some of these people are misguided philosophers. Others are educators, playing the role of sucker, who've lost their way and bought into the truthy nonsense of these fallen philosophers. Truthfully, their ideas might be labeled either truthy or postmodern. *Truthiness and postmodernism are roughly equivalent. They're both poison for education if they're taken seriously. And neither postmodernism nor truthiness helps us solve educational problems.*

Herein we find two intensely irreconcilable ideas: (1) the truth is whatever you think sounds good or is consistent with your gut feeling because there is no single truth, thereby *truthiness*; or (2) the truth is something objectively verifiable, common (or shared) knowledge, which we might call scientific *truth*. Some educators buy into truthiness—the philosophy that objectivity doesn't exist, that there is no verifiable truth about anything. They say the truth "floats," presumably on the currents of fancy, that there are only multiple and equally valid truths. In believing this, they make a mockery of education.

How can this be? *Sad and funny but true, the nonsense of truthiness is all the rage among way too many educators.* It's like they've caught a bad bug from philosophers and literary critics. But we don't have to catch it.

Truth vs. truthiness

Let's start with the idea of truth. Truth is an old word and an old idea. If you search the Internet for "truth," you'll find a lot of information and discussion of the idea and the word. Mostly you'll find there's great difficulty in defining truth and that we often engage in philosophical discussion of its true nature, something philosophers have been debating for thousands of years.[1] Yet, some of its definitions seem commonsensical. For example, Abraham Lincoln is said to have asked, "How many legs does a dog have if you call the tail a leg?" His answer, "Four; calling a tail a leg doesn't make it a leg."[2] In other words, an assertion or suggestion doesn't make truth. Abraham Lincoln may actually have said something like this in the middle of

the nineteenth-century, but that doesn't mean the issue is settled. As we shall see, the comedy-derived word *truthiness* now replaces the ages-old idea that there is no single truth about anything, only multiple truths constructed by individuals, no common knowledge but only personal knowledge.[3]

Among the meanings of truth is one related to its scientific understanding. In *Candor and Perversion: Literature, Education, and the Arts*, Roger Shattuck says, "A real world of material things, sometimes called nature, exists around us. Nature includes us, and we share it imperfectly with one another through perception, action, memory, language, love, and wonder."[4] This emphasis on nature and the natural world, on what most of us see and believe to be the real world, and on what science tells us about it are all recurring themes in what we know as the Enlightenment.

The Enlightenment or scientific tradition really got off the ground in the eighteenth century. Enlightenment science is based on the assumption that empirical evidence obtained with the greatest possible objectivity and subjected to independent and rigorous peer review is used to determine truth. We might make the following assumptions about Enlightenment truth:

- It's determined by scientific evidence, not by gut feelings or consensus. Scientists may, indeed, arrive at a consensus about data regarding a phenomenon, but the data about the phenomenon determine the truth, not the consensus.

- It can be checked out and can be falsified. As Albert Einstein may have said of his scientific ideas (at least supposedly, and the statement describes an attitude toward evidence widely shared by scientists), "No amount of experimentation can ever prove me right; a single experiment can prove me wrong."[5]

- If an idea can't be proved wrong, then scientists don't work with it. That is, if you can't conduct an experiment to test the hypothesis, and the outcome could go either way (yes or no, true or false, confirm or disconfirm), then the evidence isn't considered scientific.

Go to books written by philosophers of our day to find out how they define truth. You can find philosophers of just about every opinion, and some have written things that I find nonsensical, silly, and ultimately destructive of the very foundations of moral thought and action, and inconsistent with any kind of practical application to everyday life. Two philosophers who do address issues of truth and moral deliberation—

who make good sense and whose books have important implications for everyday decisions—are Simon Blackburn and Susan Neiman. And they argue clearly that making good, practical, morally defensible decisions requires that we accept the Enlightenment notion of truth.[6]

Here's an example of how truth in the Enlightenment sense should apply to schools. We might wonder when teaching kids to read, if method A is better than B, if the opposite is true, or if they're equally effective. Now imagine that method A is direct instruction and method B whole language. How can we determine which is better? We could just go with our gut feeling that A is better (or vice versa), or say that because most teachers we know think it is so, that A is better (or vice versa). Or, we could say the truth is that B is better than A because an authority (a school administrator or a professor of education) says so. But those gut-based or consensus-based or authority-based ways of trying to find the truth aren't scientific. The scientific approach to finding which method is better requires testing—comparing their results in a carefully designed experiment and assuming that the truth is indicated by the evidence.

The Enlightenment's scientific notion of truth is very different from *truthiness*, a word, by the way, invented by comedian Stephen Colbert. (He also invented *wikiality* to describe how truth is determined by what most people think rather than by objective facts.) Search the Internet for the term truthiness, and you'll find this definition:

1. truthiness (noun)

1: "truth that comes from the gut, not books" (Stephen Colbert, Comedy Central's *The Colbert Report*, October 2005)

2: "the quality of preferring concepts or facts one wishes to be true, rather than concepts or facts known to be true" (American Dialect Society, January 2006)[7]

Definition #1 suggests that facts are unimportant, but definition #2 is more relevant here. While Stephen Colbert may have quipped that truthiness doesn't come from books, it is nonetheless true that books aren't the sole source of truth, nor are they always truthful. We find many books full of twaddle. Some contain false information or misrepresent reality. So in spite of the fact that books may generally be more reliable than the Internet as a source of truth, don't believe everything you read.[8]

Unhappily, it appears that much of what we read and discuss about education could readily be termed "truthy" in the sense of the second definition—based on opinion, wish, or fantasy rather than on what is scientifically demonstrated to be true. In many ways, truthiness corresponds to ideas about truth and science that have come to be known as "postmodernism." Defining postmodernism is difficult. As postmodernists Usher and Edwards state, "Although it is customary to define what one is writing about, in the case of 'postmodernism' this is neither entirely possible nor entirely desirable."[9] Note also that Usher and Edwards' book is about postmodernism in education! The basic ideas of postmodernism aren't merely notions held by philosophers. They're ideas we have to contend with in schools.

Unintelligibility appears to be a basic and highly valued characteristic of many postmodernists. As I understand postmodernism, it is characterized by the following propositions:[10]

1. All truth and all knowledge are constructed according to social rules. These rules give someone power to identify truth or knowledge. Moreover, these rules have been constructed by oppressive power structures, mainly by white, European, heterosexual males, to protect their own power.

2. There are multiple truths, multiple realities, but no one or best way of knowing anything. All "truth" is merely a "text"; the text or script can be rewritten to suit one's fancy or to manipulate power. That is, power comes from deconstructing or constructing texts. Power comes from what some postmodernists refer to as "textuality." (Confused yet? I am!)

3. No text has superiority or power over another; or, at least, no text should be seen as superior or be allowed to have power over another. Truth and knowledge are nothing more than social constructs that can be deconstructed and reconstructed to suit one's desire for gaining power or passing it on to others.

4. Rationality and intelligibility are not legitimate tests of truth because rationality and intelligibility are themselves social constructs reflecting white male and Western scientific biases and lust for power.

5. Any argument that arguments 1–4 are wrong is, itself, erroneous. Truthy or postmodern views cannot be refuted on logical grounds or by any evidence, as these views of text and power are the bedrock of postmodern "theory" or "philosophy," which seems to

be saying that no text is intelligible and no individual is even the author of a text.

One must wonder then why postmodern writings have bylines, even more why postmodern writers receive royalties!

You are excused if these propositions leave you puzzled, but postmodernism defies clear and crisp definition. This has one advantage: it makes great material for humorists. Garrison Keillor, for example, makes fun of it often on his radio show. Its puffery, its pretense of intellectual honesty, its cloying treatment of truth is laughable—it makes me want to ask those who take it seriously, "Why, when you say 'no text is intelligible' should I then believe what *you write*?"

If you think this truth/truthiness business is just philosophical stuff not related to education, read on. It's directly related to what happens in lots of fields of study, including education. Even in the field of literary criticism, where it has its most fervent defenders, it's been the butt of jokes by mystified but amused observers. The send-up of postmodern literary criticism by Frederick Crews in his book *Postmodern Pooh* (as in Winnie the Pooh) is witheringly funny.[11] Try telling someone about a typical postmoderist piece of writing and you'll have to add humorist Dave Barry's signature caveat, "*I'm not making this up!*" It's that bizarre. Yet some educators are serious about making postmodernism the basis for teaching kids and training teachers!

Postmodernism relies on convoluted arguments and prizes the very convolutions needed to define it. In education, as in other fields, "hermeneutics," "cultural studies," "post-structuralism," "deconstructionism," "post-disciplinary," "anti-disciplinary," and a variety of other new-age cognitive peculiarities with similarly mysterious labels mean roughly the same thing. Some writers try to draw distinctions among the various terms, but those too are largely unintelligible. Often, postmodernists grudgingly accept someone else's use of a label but insist their views can't be categorized. Or, they may simply say their views have been mislabeled.[12] A postmodernist writer once responded to my negative review of a manuscript submitted for publication in a professional education journal. The writer denied being a postmodernist and instead insisted on being called a Gadamerian hermeneuticist.[13] Okay. Noted. All the same to me, but it sounds like the job description of the character over in the corner of the famous *Star Wars* bar scene.

The salient point here is that postmodernism and its equivalents, by whatever label, deny the existence of objective truth.[14] They all seem to correspond roughly to the comedic concept of truthiness, in that the things one wishes to be true are preferred to concepts or facts that have been proven true on the basis of scientific evidence.

Truth and truthiness: implications for education

Wow! Talk about a "belief system" that puts the kibosh on educating kids and their teachers in any responsible way! Take a minute to ponder further on these postmodernist beliefs and try to imagine their consequences for education at every level. As a basis for educating teachers, postmodernism is particularly vicious. It's vicious because it rejects the insights that science can offer, embracing only the ideologies of "power relations," "poststructuralism," "feminism," and the idea that teachers don't need to master anything other than the ideology. You don't believe it? Then read an article published in, of all places, the *Journal of Teacher Education* in 2005. In that article, Sharon Ryan and Susan Grieshaber write that "A postmodern teacher education involves moving away from this mastery model [here, they've noted, apparently without realizing it, that some people believe teachers may actually need particular knowledge and skills] to an examination of how knowledge creates boundaries and possibilities."[15] Postmodern teacher education reduces all attempts to educate students to a numbingly simple political equation that states, "all teaching interactions exercise power so that some children are empowered whereas others are not."[16]

Postmodernism embraces the view that teachers don't need to master particular areas of knowledge, specific skills related to strong instruction, or sensible behavior management strategies to be good teachers. They only need to understand the nefarious exercise of power that effective, scientifically based instruction—their stated enemy—represents! "Wait a minute, you're exaggerating," you might think to yourself. I wish I were. Brace yourself again. I did not make up the following statement about teacher education.

> For those who believe that special education practices should be informed by this kind of [empirical] scientific research, good teacher preparation is a matter of training teachers to use research in practice. Conversely, those who question the utility of this version of scientific research maintain that such an approach to teacher preparation actually precludes sound teaching practices.[17]

Hold on, here! Teaching teachers to use empirical scientific research actually *precludes* sound teaching practices? Others of us have concluded that this kind of stuff that passes for "thinking" wrecks teacher education.[18]

In the end, postmodernism offers nothing to teach—other than passing along the postmodernists' fantastical views on knowledge, power, and oppression. We should find this laughable. It's funny, but it's also tragic because some people treat this babble as serious educational philosophy and actually promote it.

Teachers have a terrible time teaching anything when the truth can't be determined. Postmodernists might indoctrinate, but they can't teach. And they won't even be very good at indoctrination, much less teaching, without the competencies—the knowledge and skills—that they need to be good teachers. You also might conclude that many of the arguments of postmodernists are extraordinarily banal—boringly obvious. For example, postmodernism may suggest that the effect of a poem or novel depends on both the writer's intention and the reader's interpretation of it.[19] Nobody can argue with this; we have known this for decades, if not centuries. Or postmodernism might suggest science can't answer every question one might ask. Again, no argument. Not a new insight. But more to the point, in no case does postmodernism add important insights into the human condition, show us the way to figure things out with better results, or tell us what should be done to make people's lives better.

All of us, regardless of the nature of specific criticisms about schools, want improved education, including safer schools, fairer opportunities for all students, better teachers, higher achievement, more balanced emphasis on various aspects of the curriculum, and more efficient operation. We want to make students' lives better, not just address personal pleasures with the parlor games of postmodernism. The issue isn't so much *what* we want, since few would disagree with the goal of improving students' lives, as *how* we can do it. Regarding how to do it, there are two distinct perspectives: truth and truthiness. I think truth has a lot more to offer educators than truthiness for reasons that may by now be obvious. Still, those of us who care about kids and schools have to contend with postmodern nonsense and the people who spout it.

I know, like, and respect as individuals quite a few of those who have embraced what might be called either postmodernism or truthiness in education, but I don't agree with their take on the nature of truth.

In fact, I find what they say both humorous (in a dark way) and sad. And I chuckle at their suggestion that I (or anyone else) should believe what they say about truth when the primary postmodern premise is that there is no truth or that truth is a personal, gut-based thing that can't be verified empirically, objectively, or scientifically. To paraphrase Mark Twain's conclusion about Christian Science, the postmodernists' position that we should believe them when they say truth can't be established objectively is an ideological oxymoron that radically modifies the value of their reasoning.

Mark Twain wrote a particularly apropos maxim: "It is wiser to find out than to suppose."[20] Science is our best tool for finding things out, and using it requires logical, linear thinking and skepticism about assertions. The disconnect between the hard and fast rules of science and the elastic "rules" of postmodernism couldn't be more absolute. And that disconnect has been noted for a long time. It's time for twenty-first-century educators to wake up and smell the coffee!

Historical notes related to postmodernism/truthiness

I'm reminded of an observation by two nineteenth-century physicians who were early psychiatrists. Drs. Francis Stribling and Edward Jarvis were skeptical of an almost universally accepted assumption of that time—that masturbation caused insanity. In 1842, Stribling suggested in his *Annual Reports of the Court of Directors of the Western Lunatic Asylum to the Legislature of Virginia* that perhaps masturbation wasn't, after all, the cause of insanity. It was a logical error, he noted, to assume that because insane people seemed to masturbate frequently, it was the cause of their insanity.[21] (This is a nice reference to a well-known error of logic—assuming an occurrence was caused by what preceded it or, in Latin, the logical fallacy *"post hoc ergo propter hoc."*) A decade later, in 1852, Dr. Jarvis, writing in the *American Journal of Insanity* (later to become the *American Journal of Psychiatry*), wisely noted that masturbation couldn't be said on the basis of any scientific data to be the cause of an increase in insanity because although there was a marked increase in the incidence of insanity at that time, and while mental patients did masturbate, there were no studies to show a connection. His conclusion was, "we have no means of knowing whether masturbation increases or diminishes."[22] Good thinking, Dr. Jarvis! Although Stribling and Jarvis were primitives by today's scientific standards, at least they had the idea of finding truth through empirical means. They were reasonable skeptics and found

the truthiness of their day unconvincing. Sometimes, yesterday's science becomes today's superstition. Science is always evolving, improving, never perfect, and it can be wrong. It has been many times. Nevertheless, it remains the only self-correcting method of discovery that places a premium on reliable data obtained with the least bias and the greatest objectivity. Although biases and preferences can never be totally eliminated, the rigors of scientific discipline will continue to require subjecting a claim to a particularly harsh and objective scrutiny.[23] When a given bias isn't subjected to such scrutiny, then the claim will eventually be exposed as not having been tested in a scientific manner. This is the fatal flaw of postmodernists: while they seem to recognize that biases and preferences exist, they fail to subject their own personal views to harsh scrutiny; they accept them as defining realities.

Nor do the few other alternative approaches to scientific knowledge offer hope of finding a common understanding of reality that is central to social justice, fairness, and equity. And that is essential for responsible education. Postmodernists have shut themselves off from common (scientific) knowledge. Without finding the common, we have two choices, both of which are unacceptable: we can either (1) *avoid* or (2) *dominate* those who are different from us—unless we simply don't believe common understandings are important, that they aren't the glue that holds societies together, or that they aren't critical for formulating effective educational strategies. Attempts to teach tolerance, for example, that are without a foundation of common understanding to show why it's an essential concept haven't worked. More importantly, without Enlightenment thinking one has no real basis for moral thinking or for finding what might be called moral clarity.[24]

Truthiness in education: an example

Spending money with truthiness as a guide isn't wise for anyone, especially an educator. Remember that truthiness and postmodernism rely on what "feels" right or is in line with what one wishes or hopes or asserts is true, not on science or empirical evidence. Here's a story to illustrate the point:

> *George Howard, a university professor, read in the local paper that a neighboring school system had invested thousands of dollars to hire professors from a university in another state to teach their teachers to use "cooperative learning," a method of getting students to work together. Cooperative learning was to be implemented in this district with the entire school population, in*

every classroom, kindergarten through high school. The money was used to purchase summer instruction for teachers and ongoing workshops throughout the year.

After reading the newspaper article, George called the superintendent of this school system and offered to test the effectiveness of cooperative learning at no cost to the schools. George had a large group of advanced graduate students who would assist him, and he thought that his offer would be a boon to the school system as well as a benefit to his students, who would learn about program evaluation by applying their research skills to an actual problem. Imagine his surprise when the superintendent said to him, "Absolutely not, Professor Howard. We've invested a lot of money in this thing already. If it doesn't work, we don't want to know about it. Besides, no research is ever going to convince me that it works or it doesn't. We don't need research to tell us what's right."

George laughed immediately when the superintendent said this. He thought the superintendent was joking. Then he realized that there was dead silence on the phone. He later said to me, "My God! Wouldn't you want to know whether an expensive program requiring massive reorganization of your school system is effective? But the superintendent was serious. He didn't want to know whether it worked and didn't think anybody could find out!"

This superintendent obviously didn't want to find the truth. He already had truthiness, which he apparently mistook for truth. Ideologies like his—beliefs that defy empirical evidence—undoubtedly account for much wasteful spending in education. But it does more than sanction waste. It encourages chicanery not only in education but in politics and every other aspect of life as well.

Additional chicanery

Postmodernism's effects on education are bad enough. But education isn't the only casualty of postmodern philosophy. It's even provided a smoke screen for murder, as indicated in a report by David Grann published in the *The New Yorker* on February 11 and 18, 2008.[25] Oh, wait! Murder? The facts of the case in Grann's article suggest that the subject of the report is guilty of murder. But, after all, if there is no objective reality, then someone can deny anything, including murder or the cause of AIDS.[26] Amazing, indeed, but postmodernism is a way of thinking that's bought into by many people who should know better. It's candy for politicians who claim that whatever they say is, by definition, truth. It's perfect for the educational quack.

Those who embrace truthiness and postmodernism rather than science or Enlightenment thinking insist they discriminate among statements or ideas. They do, apparently, believe that in some cases A is better than B. But, they refuse to state the criteria for making these discriminations, for deciding how A is better than B.[27] There is one notable exception, of course: the truthy or postmodern view is superior to the "outdated" scientific view because, as postmodernists repeatedly imply, all truth is simply made up. Never mind the cognitive cul de sac of this argument, from which the only exit is a U-turn. Somehow this lethal self-contradiction is acceptable to proponents of truthiness or postmodernism. Never mind, either, that since truth is made by power—a favorite postmodern cognitive gimmick—the powerful, including elected leaders and dictators alike, can just make up their own version of the "truth" to suit their purposes. You have to give up the notion of speaking truth to power when you buy into the idea that power makes truth. Imagine trying to make the case to a parent whose child has a disability, while as a postmodernist your assumption is that since there's no truth, the child's disability can't be proven or determined in any objective way.

I like Roger Shattuck's comment that he hopes all intellectuals who embrace postmodernism and believe that we must abandon all hope of objective fact and truth pull jury duty, in which facts and truth really matter for achieving social justice.[28] I also admire columnist Colbert King's clear writing, including his unapologetic assumptions that (1) there are truths and there are lies about people and events, and (2) we can discriminate between truths and lies. The fact that Dr. Tareq Tahboub of Jordan wrote certain things about Condoleezza Rice when she was national security advisor doesn't mean they're true. In fact, King claims that what Dr. Tahboub wrote in an Arabic-language daily paper was "full of lies and misrepresentations," and King presents the evidence to substantiate the charge.[29]

Truthiness and postmodernism: not good for fixing educational problems

It's a fair question whether truth or truthiness—science or postmodernism—is more helpful in solving education's problems. I found in my own teaching that applying the principles derived from behavioral science was generally successful. More significantly, in my doctoral studies in special education at the University of Kansas I learned from research literature that a scientific approach to behavior, though less than perfect, is our best bet for trying to help kids behave appropriately and learn academic skills. Most important of all, I learned the power of the organized skepticism that we call science. Science plays an indispensable role in helping children with exceptionalities and their families. It's also indispensable in teaching others how to help children and adults most effectively.

I was reared in a very religious environment, so I'm aware of how personal beliefs can influence perceptions. I was made aware at an early age of the limitations of science in addressing human problems. You can be skeptical of science, too, and from an early age I was steeped in skepticism about scientific understanding. As an adult, I retain the view that some issues can't be resolved by science or be addressed completely by scientific methods. Nevertheless, I also value the insights that science can provide about many things. Unwillingness to seek and yield to available scientific evidence is morally reprehensible narrow-mindedness. Refusing to use science to find out how to help people more effectively epitomizes moral turpitude, especially when such refusal is based on philosophical dithering about the nature of truth.

But this is just personal testimonial.[30] For other views on the value of scientific evidence in all manner of work and moral judgment, consult the work of others.[31] You will have to decide for yourself whether truth or truthiness is better trusted. Truthiness does have the advantage of allowing you to deny anything at all—even the connection between HIV and AIDS.[32] With truthiness, you can wish away whatever you don't like and wish into existence whatever you do. With truthiness, you can wish away a child's disability—but remember that a school administrator can wish it away, too. With truthiness, a child's disability is just your opinion, which is no better than anyone else's.

In a sense, the choice between truthiness and truth is a choice between style and substance. Truthiness is cute and appealing; truth is often harder to swallow. But more than style is involved. What makes us feel good is often a form of truthiness that might be called "kitsch." But, as philosopher Susan Neiman put it, "Kitsch is much more than a question of style; it's a preference for consolation over truth."[33]

The tragicomedy of truthiness in education

The poor thinking known as truthiness is a major obstacle when trying to improve our schools. Truthiness is easy. It lets us say and believe anything we want about schools and schooling. Truth is harder. It requires careful analysis of evidence and of ideas.

The unfortunate truth is some people don't consider poor thinking poor thinking. To them, nothing can be more than truthy. Injected into education, this intellectual perversion creates disaster. This may make us want to cry. First, we should laugh at the very idea of truthiness.

Notes for Chapter Two

[1] Blackburn (2005)

[2] Hesse (2008) points out that the attribution of these particular words to Abraham Lincoln is false but that Lincoln did, in fact, say something similar about cows. See also web address for endnotes, wisdomquotes.

[3] See Backburn (2005), Gross, Levitt, & Lewis (1996), and Hecht (2003) for further discussion

[4] Shattuck (1999, pp. 4–6)

[5] See web address for wisdomquotes

[6] Blackburn (2005), Neiman (2008)

[7] See web address for Merriam-Webster

[8] Hesse (2008) noted the difficulties in finding truth and reported that some college students and instructors see books as a source of reliable information. However, you might note that a book by Harry and Klingner (2006) and a 2007 article by the same authors contain statements about special education for children with emotional and behavioral disorders that are simply incorrect according to many other sources of information, including a book they cite in support of their misinformation (see Kauffman, Mock, & Simpson, 2007 for discussion).

[9] Usher & Edwards (1994, p. 6)

[10] Postmodernism is discussed further in many sources, including Kauffman & Sasso (2006a, 2006b), Koertge (1998), Mostert, Kavale, & Kauffman (2008), Sasso (2007), and Sokal & Bricmont (1998). For a report on how postmodernism might work out in literature, see Grann (2008).

[11] See Crews (2001)

[12] See Pillow (2000)

[13] Gadamerian, presumably, because the views were patterned on those of H. Gadamer; see Gadamer (1959/1988)

[14] Dasenbrock (1995)

[15] Ryan & Grieshaber (2005, p. 36)

[16] Ryan & Grieshaber (2005, p. 43)

[17] Gallagher (2004, p. 4)

[18] Kauffman, Mock, Mostert, & Kavale (2008)

[19] See Conquest (2000, p. 222)

[20] Mark Twain Foundation (1976, p. 943)

[21] Stribling (1842)

[22] Jarvis (1852, p. 354)

[23] See Feynman (1998, 1999), Gould (1997a, 1997b, 2000), Gross (1998), Shermer (1997, 2001), Tolson (1998), Wilson (1998)

[24] Neiman (2008)

[25] Grann (2008)

[26] Specter (2007)

[27] Kauffman & Sasso (2006b)

[28] Shattuck (1999, p. 94)

[29] King (2001, p. A29)

[30] For more on my own views of science and reason, see, for example, Kauffman (1999, 2003b), Kauffman, Mock, Mostert, & Kavale (2008), Kauffman & Sasso (2006a, 2006b)

[31] For more on the views of others regarding science and reason, see, for example, Blackburn (2005), Detrich, Keyworth, & States (2008), Feynman (1998, 1999), Gould (1996, 1997a, 1997b, 2000), Gross (1998), Gross & Levitt (1998), Gross, Levitt, & Lewis (1996), Jacobson, Mulick, & Foxx (2005), Koertge (1998), Morris & Mather (2008), Neiman (2008), Shermer (1997, 2001), Sokal & Bricmont (1998), Tolson (1998), and Wilson (1998)

[32] See Specter (2007)

[33] Neiman (2008, p. 425)

Part I
Laughing and Crying

Chapter Three:
The Art of Poor Thinking

How the Art of Poor Thinking Is Practiced with Tragicomic Effects on Education

It's imperative for teachers as well as parents not to be tricked by rhetoric that conceals poor thinking about education. Occasionally, poor thinking is accidental. When it's accidental, it's usually regretted and results in embarrassment and apology. Sometimes, though, poor thinking is used purposely to fool others. It might be used for fun by a comedian or as part of a sales pitch or a con game by a clever person who is fully aware of the deception. Hoodwinking others may be a legitimate part of the arts of comedy, merchandising, politics, and even academics, but when used for purely personal gain it can be harmful on a number of levels. *When it's used in talk of education, artful bad thinking is tragicomic.*

Eight artful ploys

Understanding how poor thinking is used artfully for personal profit allows us to avoid it more easily. Here are eight ways people practice the art of hoodwinking others for fame or profit:

1. Insert enough truth to catch people's attention.

2. Assume people won't thoroughly examine the underlying idea.

3. Use outliers (atypical cases) as examples of the typical.

4. Assert that the average represents all.

5. Make personal testimony more convincing than reliable research.

6. Find a way to deride more reasonable propositions.

7. Overcomplicate simple things or oversimplify complex things.

8. Combine any of these or add other half-baked ideas into a potpourri and peddle as a panacea.

1: Use a partial truth

A partial truth is more difficult to overcome than a total lie. For this reason, in a court of law we swear to tell "the truth, the whole truth, and nothing but the truth." A partial truth creates a myth, which

is then distanced from reality by overgeneralization, distortion, or misapplication of fact. Partial truths are as damaging as complete untruths, if not more so. And people often are fooled by partial truths when they wouldn't be by something completely untrue. So, for example, if someone says, "Public schools are failing" (some are), the whole truth (some are and some aren't) is harder to defend than an utter lie like, "No public school is successful by any standard." The same is true for sweeping half-truths like, "Special education is a failure" (it often is), when the whole truth is that it's often better than general education and sometimes it's truly a success.

2: Assume people won't think carefully

The assumption that people aren't going to think much about what you say is usually safe. In fact, it's the very foundation for most ploys—slogans, for example. The title character of John Irving's 1989 novel, *A Prayer for Owen Meany* (whose voice was always represented by capital letters), would say that things of this sort are MADE FOR TELEVISION! That is, they're made for unthinking responses, demanding we put our intelligence on hold. For example, in response to a frequent plug we hear on public radio, "Think in ideas" (as if there's any other way to think), Owen Meany's signature dismissal would be apropos.

People who make witless statements seem to be betting no one will seriously question what they say or write. They don't see a need to formulate simple questions about slogans like "All children can learn." These sloganeers don't think anyone's going to ask questions about an actual child like, "What can he learn?" "How long will it take her to learn it?" "How much would their learning cost us?" The typical user of nonsense verbiage may even add a redundant qualifier like, "And all means *all*," without concern that someone might ask, "By all, then, do you mean *each and every* child, *no* exceptions?" The reality is that people in every walk of life, including school board members, legislators, business executives, and politicians, too often disconnect their powers of reason when confronted by problems in public education. And this is even worse when it comes to special education. Slipshod thinking on this scale explains why public education is indeed a tragicomedy whose sad plot unfolds daily in clear view of us all—well, at least most.

3: Consider outliers typical

Using outliers—exceptions to the rule—as examples of the typical assumes people won't question variables in human nature, won't understand statistical distributions[1] or will deny their existence and relevancy. (Statistical distributions are often depicted by a graph or curve, usually much like a normal bell-shaped curve or a positive segment of a sine curve.) We've seen tobacco companies use outliers to illustrate the non-effects of smoking on health. A Marlboro Man strides the small screen or billboard, a rugged outdoorsman who has smoked for years but remains in robust health. He refutes the science that says smoking is unhealthful, that it has severe consequences on respiratory and circulatory well-being. Or active, attractive young people are shown smoking, as if it's not a risk to their health. We know there are those who smoked heavily for years, yet lived long and healthful lives, but that outlier doesn't change hard numbers, the statistics, that clearly show how greatly they increased their risk of heart or lung disease. Tobacco executives have also used outliers to point out how some lung cancer victims who've never smoked prove smoking doesn't cause lung cancer. This example lies at the other extreme of a statistical distribution. Yet statistics couldn't be more clear: smoking substantially increases the risk of getting vascular or lung disease or both.

In education, too, deceptive claims are often based on statistical outliers. Apply this kind of thinking to special education, and bingo, an exceptional student who does well in general education can be said to illustrate how full inclusion can work for *every* exceptional child. Or the errant identification of a *few* students misplaced in special education is said to show how there shouldn't be *any* students placed in special education. Con artists cite the example of the child who learns to read with no instruction at all, or *some* who learn to read despite poor instruction that fails *most kids* by third grade. These outliers are then used to defend worthless instructional practices.

Another example is the discounting of a proven-effective instructional approach because of the failure of a few children. Several such wholly unrepresentative cases have been used by those touting a personal, often hidden, agenda to promote ineffective instructional methods that are then adopted and promoted to replace effective ones.

Instructional methods aren't the only educational arena in which outliers are used to make absurd arguments. Extraordinary teachers who overcome outrageous odds—lack of instructional materials, crumbling buildings, large class size, extremely low pay—to produce

exceptional outcomes are cited as models for what all teachers should be able to do on a dime and a prayer. The same outlier is then twisted to show that the lack of resources in the previous example shows teachers can operate effectively without them. With this logic, teachers who don't achieve good student outcomes despite small classes, high salaries, and limitless access to instructional materials are then used as distorted examples to prove these resources aren't essential.

The point is, we can be easily fooled by two types of statistics: (1) when outliers are used as examples of the typical, or (2) when the typical is used as an example of extreme outliers. In short, outliers don't prove much of anything about the typical.

4: Claim the average applies to all

Said differently, using the typical as representative of *everyone* in the statistical distribution is the opposite of using outliers as examples of the typical. Stephen J. Gould explained in his book *Full House* why everyone in a distribution should be considered, but he doesn't mean outliers can or should be used as examples of the typical. Gould should know—he exemplified the atypical. He lived 30 times longer than the average for people with his kind of cancer—240 months when the average was only 8![2]

In education, the typical is too often used to represent all students or all cases. Whenever someone suggests all students should learn this or that, we hope *all* will not be taken literally. The rhetoric of some reformers discounts the needs of kids whose cognitive capacity or behavioral control is way below that of their typical age mates, or that of kids whose intellectual power or virtuosity in some area of performance is way above that of their age peers. The average applies to schools and teachers as well. Is American public education failing, or is it a remarkable success? What about special education? Depending on how we define success or failure, we could make the case that the public schools aren't doing a very good job, or that they're doing a superb job. We could conclude that special education is a miserable failure or a smashing success. But in either case, the general conclusion—that they're somewhere in between—avoids those at the extremes: if we conclude schools are failing, it ignores those that are successful; if the conclusion is that schools are successful, it must deny the existence of those failing.

Truthful and helpful talk about public education recognizes that almost nothing ever applies to "all" cases—that is, to each and every one. And

exceptions should never be used to reject educational programs that are proven effective for most. On the other hand, the rhetoric that rules out all exceptions to focus solely on the typical is equally destructive and often serves as the basis for such misbegotten policies as zero tolerance, in which the same rule is applied to all cases regardless of extenuating circumstances.[3]

So, what can or should be expected or demanded of *all* students, meaning each and every one? Not much, in my opinion, because the variation among students is so dramatic and significant. Maybe "doing your best" or "learning all you can" would be appropriate for literally all, but "your best" is difficult to define, and "best" is a concept that some learners with low cognitive ability don't understand. And "learning all you can" will drive some children with already high motivation to work too hard. However, if we were able to find agreement on the meaning of these unclear terms, and determine together that "all children" really means the great majority, not every single child, then a core curriculum, a standard set of expectations, might make sense.[4]

5: Rely on personal testimony, not research

A common trick of marketers is to compare research-based results unfavorably to those from personal experience or testimony. For example, a pain reliever commercial features a man who says he doesn't care what studies show, he knows what works for him. Whatever you might want to say about this, it's certainly an artful ploy! Unfortunately, it's also a popular tactic used in educational rhetoric.

The belief that educational research is without value when compared to personal testimony has, unfortunately, a long history in education. True, the science of education isn't the same as the science of chemistry or physics (or any of the other "hard" or natural sciences), but this doesn't mean educators can't practice the skepticism that's the foundation of the hard sciences. Nor does it mean educators shouldn't depend on evidence gleaned from good science on education in which hypotheses are tested the way they should be, scientifically. The science of education is much like (and closely related to) the science of psychology. Much education—and much psychology—is *not* science, and in both fields there are some practitioners who reject science and scientific knowledge. Still, the basics of scientific inquiry apply as surely to challenges in education as to any other field of knowledge.

6: Deride reasonable ideas

Scientific inquiry requires trying to figure out where an argument could end up. But anyone can, if so motivated, drive a reasonable proposition into the ground. In *Why People Believe Weird Things*, Michael Shermer describes the argument known as *reductio ad absurdum*—"carrying the argument to its logical end and so reducing it to an absurd conclusion."[5] Closely related is the "slippery slope" trope, that once you take the first step in one direction, you start an irreversible slide toward its endpoint. Shermer uses this example to illustrate the fallacy of slippery slope logic: if you eat one scoop of high-fat ice cream, you will wind up morbidly obese and dying prematurely of heart disease. Sometimes people who take that first slippery step do slide all the way down. Usually, they don't. In special education, this logic has been applied, for example, to placement of exceptional children, so that to disallow the inclusion (in general education) of one child, is to lose the purity of full inclusion and to initiate the fall to total exclusion.

Sometimes, as Shermer also notes, it's useful to follow a hypothesis to its logical conclusion to see if it makes a valid point. More often, though, this only yields unacceptable and absurd results and the most extreme of "solutions," for example, suicide as the solution to depression. Taking something to its logical extreme becomes, as historian Robert Conquest puts it in his book *Reflections on a Ravaged Century*, not just another idea to be evaluated, but an *IDEA* (not the Individuals with Disabilities Education Act's IDEA, but a thought, principle, or ideology) to be served at any cost, even the loss of rationality.[6] By driving a reasonable proposition into the ground, we can arrive at all manner of extreme, rationally untenable, and destructive positions on a variety of issues. The *IDEA* becomes a matter of faith, a position held with religious fervor.

Among the most interesting of life's questions is this one: how do people become radicalized, so that judgment and reason go out the window? How do people become terrorists and murderers in defense of an ideology? Maybe they start with a reasonable proposition and are rewarded by the adulation of others for taking increasingly extreme views on a particular issue. Perhaps it's a form of madness we'll never fully understand. Whatever causes it, the extreme requires abandoning judgment in favor of an absolute. An example is the *IDEA* of full inclusion—it demands adherence to faith that the general or regular classroom is *always* best, regardless of any evidence to the contrary.

But, human judgment is less than perfect. This is why sensible people object to slippery slope speculation, the belief that if we allow *any* judgment or wiggle room they'll lose everything. The truth is that *any* and *every* slope is slippery. The alternative is making things cut-and-dried. You may be tempted to conclude that one judgment is as good as another if we don't adopt an absolute position. But just because we allow judgment—we judge one evil or good against another—doesn't mean that judgment must be accepted willy-nilly. Judgment is required to distinguish good from bad, and I think it's usually bad judgment to exclude human judgment in the individual case. Relying on judgment does allow the possibility of evil, while disallowing judgement ensures evil. As philosopher Susan Neiman concludes about moral clarity, "It means working to make sense of things you do not even want to acknowledge. It often means not knowing if you ever get it right."[7]

There is the myth that scientists are certain of many things. But scientists, when questioned, also often reply, "That depends." We try to teach children to think things through, which means, if we're successful, they'll also often reply to a question by saying, "That depends," showing they too understand the folly of absolutism. Absolutism and tragicomedy are cut from the same cloth. Perhaps some seek comforting simplicity to escape irresolvable complexity.

7: Overcomplicate the simple or oversimplify the complex

Overcomplication of simple things is funny in its pomposity, but it's truly maddening to those who look for readily understandable language about simple things. Richard Feynman gave us a funny description of the overcomplication of language by a sociologist in a paper written for an interdisciplinary conference. Feynman says that he couldn't make any sense at all of the sociologist's paper until he started reading one sentence at a time and translated from pompous language into plain English.

So I stopped—at random—and read the next sentence very carefully. I can't remember it precisely, but it was very close to this: "The individual member of the social community often receives his information via visual, symbolic channels." I went back and forth over it, and translated. You know what it means? "People read."

Then I went over the next sentence, and I realized that I could translate that one also. Then it became a kind of empty business: "Sometimes people read; sometimes people listen to the radio," and

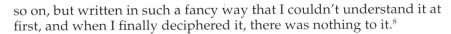

so on, but written in such a fancy way that I couldn't understand it at first, and when I finally deciphered it, there was nothing to it.[8]

Such confusion of relatively simple things by complex, dense language is commonly found in education, too. You might recall some of the examples of mumbo jumbo I gave you in Chapter 1. Consider this statement: "Situating knowledge then involves examining the historical, social, political, economic, and cultural contexts that have given rise to various understandings and practices associated with the education of young children"[9] might be interpreted to mean . . . well, I'm not really certain, but perhaps more simply (in my suggested translation) "we need to consider the origin of ideas about how to teach young children." The quotation is 29 words; my suggested translation is 14. Maybe doubling the number of words was needed to convey the idea, but I doubt it.

Conversely, people may conceal the complexity of an issue behind a veneer of simplicity. School reform rhetoric often relies on catch phrases, sort of like advertisements, that are oversimplifications of complex issues. Having "the same high expectations for all students" sounds reasonable enough, but you can see its silliness when you examine it closely. It ignores the complexity of deciding what's reasonable to expect from a student and, as importantly, what isn't. It's as unthinking as saying we should pay the same high salaries to all employees or have the same high expectations of musical or athletic performance for all individuals. For some students of any given age or grade, a given expectation (e.g., in reading) will be unreasonably high; for others, it will be too low.

Of course, those who think such statements are just great will say that they're not to be taken literally to mean that the *same* expectation should apply to all students. So, what does "the same high expectations for all students" mean? Maybe the intended meaning is merely "expect all students to make progress" or "expect all students to do their best." If so, why don't they say *that* instead? I also wonder how expecting all students to make progress or do their best is any different from what the vast majority of teachers *now* expect. They don't expect students' best efforts? If not, that's revealing. Besides, expectations without bold and robust instruction have little effect, if any, on what a student can do. It's time we give up magical thinking about expectations—thinking that if we just *expect* students to do something then they will.

8: Use other half-baked ideas or combos

Rest assured there are other ways of using poor thinking to fool people, and they can be used in any combination. Think about some other artful ploys. Someone can use an ambiguous statement from a well-known person who is (or was) intelligent about many things to support an argument that doesn't stand up to careful scrutiny. Or someone might misrepresent an idea. Sometimes they do this by omitting an important word. For example, there's the often-heard statement that "consistency is the hobgoblin of small minds," when the actual quotation of Ralph Waldo Emerson is, "A foolish consistency is the hobgoblin of little minds . . ." Oh, you mean we have to consider whether *the consistency in question* is foolish? Consistency is *sometimes* sensible? Consistency *could* be wise? Obviously, consistency *can* be silly. Sometimes, it's an indication of a weak intellect, but not always by any means. Often, it's quite the opposite.

Another amusing but deadly misrepresentation is the fractured analogy—a comparison that doesn't make sense if you stop to think about it, like between subatomic physics and human behavior. An idea might be misrepresented in a non sequitur, an inference that doesn't follow from the premises. For example, here's a non sequitur that I made up: "We know from Heisenberg's uncertainty principle (a principle in physics having to do *only* with subatomic particles) that you can't predict the behavior of children in a classroom." (More fun with Heisenberg is to come in Chapter 5.) Truth is, if you can't predict the behavior of children at all, you aren't going to be worth a nickel as a teacher.

Alan Sokal and Jean Bricmont have described in considerable detail how philosophers and social scientists often misunderstand basic principles in sciences outside their area of expertise. For example, philosophers and others working in the humanities have often botched the meanings of ideas in physics. Thus, their attempt to apply the ideas to social or interpersonal problems begins with a basic intellectual error.[10] Then they can't justifiably apply the principles to social problems. But their high-sounding talk does fool many people. Many educators, too.

Watch out for the scam!

Charlatans have lots of ways to pull people in. And combinations of strategies are often used to fool people. The art of poor thinking certainly has contributed to education's tragicomedy. When we read something that doesn't make good sense or isn't readily interpretable, we need to ask ourselves whether the problem is our intellectual capacity or an indication of the intellectual muck into which discussions of education have too often fallen. We also need to be inquisitive and honest enough to ask whether an assertion is the whole truth.

We've too often let education fall prey to scam artists. This is, to be sure, tragic. We need to become more aware of how such artists work. Before we cry, though, let's laugh at how they go about their business.

Notes for Chapter Three

[1] A statistical distribution can be thought of as a smoothed curve of a bar graph of values that we get when we measure something like height, weight, years lived after diagnosis of cancer, years lived by smokers, or academic achievement (test scores, for example).

A graph or curve depicting a distribution shows the frequency (i.e., number of people or items or events) obtaining each score or value on a measurement. The graph can be for a small group or a large one. The distribution or curve can change in some ways, but not in others (I discuss this further in Chapter 8). However, distributions often approximate a "normal" curve with the shape referred to as a "bell curve." The figure below is a bar graph and an associated smoothed curve to illustrate a hypothetical distribution of test scores for 113 individuals. The scores range from 1 to 15. The figure shows that very few individuals got extremely low or extremely high scores, but a lot got scores in the range of 6 to 11 (average and close to it). In this distribution, the mean (arithmetic average), the median (the midpoint, above which and below which there are equal numbers of cases), and the mode (the most frequent score) are all the same. The mean, median, and mode are *always* the same in a normal distribution. "Outliers" are those at the extremes (or under the "tails," high and low) of the distribution. *All* distributions have lots of typical or average cases and a small number of "outliers," those not close to the average but at the extreme high or extreme low end or tail.

Histogram (bar graph) and an associated smoothed curve illustrating a near-normal distribution.

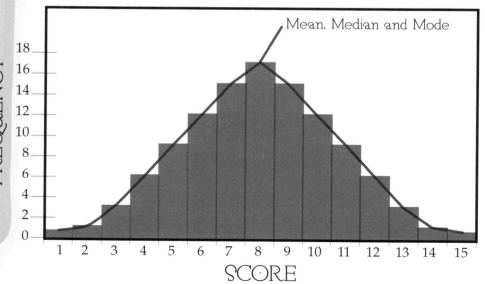

[2] Gould (1996)

[3] Skiba & Rausch (2006)

[4] For example, E. D. Hirsch's notion of what every American needs to know; see Hirsch (1987)

[5] Shermer (1997, p. 58)

[6] Conquest (2000)

[7] Neiman (2008, p. 422)

[8] Feynman (1985, pp. 281–282)

[9] Ryan & Grieshaber (2005, p. 36)

[10] Sokal & Bricmont (1998)

Part I
Laughing and Crying

Chapter Four:
Slogans and Trite Phrases

How Slogans and Trite Phrases Sabotage Common Sense and Contribute to the Tragicomedy of Education

Most slogans, catch phrases, and other kinds of trivial statements contain elements of truth. They perpetuate myths or misimpressions precisely because you can find a shard of truth in them. This is what makes a slogan or trite phrase stick, makes it attractive, and draws people into the larger falsehood.[1] Slogans are a tricky business, and the trick is to find just enough truth to fool people without telling them the whole truth. A big lie is usually sold one partial-truth at a time. Trite phrases do the same kind of snow job. And neither slogans nor trite phrases solve educational problems. They suggest a quick and easy or unthinking fix. They do sometimes make us smile or laugh, but they don't represent good thinking.

If nonthink of this kind were confined to business, marketing, and political campaigns, then it might be okay. But the trouble is that it's become common in talk of schools and, sadly, even popular among educators. So parents with children in public schools need to be particularly alert to slogans and catchy but meaningless word combinations. *And, before crying we need to laugh about the silliness of these invitations to stop thinking and let advertising agencies lead the parade.*

How slogans and trite phrases work

Slogans and catchy phrases are often put on bumper stickers, sometimes to convey what the car owner believes is a serious message, sometimes to make people laugh. On my own car, I have a sticker that says, "If evolution is outlawed, only outlaws will evolve." I think it's funny because it's a parody of the old saw about guns and outlaws. It's also amusing to "outlaw" a social judgment and at the same time a scientific principle. And it's funny to consider an evolved outlaw. What does he become: a craftier outlaw, an in-law? Another bumper sticker, one I've only imagined, would also be funny for the same reasons: "If gravity is outlawed, only outlaws will fall down."

But misleading words and trivial statements in public education are serious business. For our purposes here, I won't distinguish among slogans, catch phrases, and trivialities. They're all encouragements

not to think. You've probably run across some of these popular but meaningless words and phrases. People who talk about schools tend to use them too much.

In *The Schools We Need and Why We Don't Have Them*, E. D. Hirsch, Jr., provides a guide to these empty educational terms and phrases:

> Prospective teachers and members of the general public are bemused, bullied, and sometimes infected by seductive rhetorical flourishes like "child-centered schooling" or bullying ones like the dismissive words "drill and kill." . . . Repetition and consensus give the phrases a self-evident, not-to-be-questioned quality which induces those who repeat them to believe them earnestly and implicitly.[2]

Hirsch's list of misleading slogans and phrases is too long to reproduce in full, but it includes alarmingly vacuous language like "learning to learn," "life-long learning," "child-centered schooling," "developmentally appropriate," "learning styles," "discovery learning," "constructivism," "cooperative learning," "holistic learning," "mere facts," "teaching for understanding," "critical thinking skills," "multiple intelligences," "authentic assessment," "portfolio assessment," and many kindred neologisms, meaningless if catchy combinations of words, and trivial observations. Terms like these are now popular among educators and those who sell education to the public, including educational entrepreneurs, news people, business leaders, and politicians.

An example in education

To see how using slogans and catch phrases works when applied to education, consider this story from parents whose child with special needs was included in a general education classroom. They questioned their fifth-grade child's teacher, Natalie, on her ideas about school reform. She told them of her recent training from a "high-powered" faculty member at a university's school of education. Further, she assured them the school's top administrators and school board were instrumental in arranging her training.

> *Natalie thinks these people—the university professor and her school administrators—must know what they're talking about, and she isn't about to question them. Furthermore, she says, she's using "brain-based" methods and accommodates different "learning styles." Well, the parents think, better to base learning on the brain than some other organ! And they wonder what "style" has to do with learning basic math or reading.*

These parents, however, don't see evidence that these highly touted methods are effective. Lots of the students in Natalie's class still don't know their basic number facts—addition and multiplication tables—and can't solve simple word problems in arithmetic. Natalie says facts aren't important, that kids have calculators to give them facts any time they need them. She just wants her students to learn to make good guesses and compare them to what their calculator says. But the parents worry that when students don't know their addition and times tables they won't know if the answer on the calculator is right or wrong. Nor will they be able to tell whether they've made a mistake in what they entered. Sometimes we hit wrong keys. It's important to know when the calculator is wrong because you've made a mistake in keying something in.

Natalie says parents shouldn't be concerned, because her math curriculum has the stamp of approval of major professional organizations and the school board, as well as the superintendent and principal. Natalie assures them their son, Skip, will do just fine without learning number facts. She tells them it's more important that Skip's learning the process of finding the facts. But the parents aren't buying it.

I don't blame these parents for not buying it, even with the weight of the administration behind it. Skip's teacher, Natalie, and the district seem to have adopted the popular slogans and key words of trite statements without thinking much about them. They seem to have been carried away on a stream of verbiage with a lot of superficial glamour but little or no substance.

Many jaunty phrases don't make sense if you think about them. "All children can learn" is a familiar mantra with about as much meaning as "all children are young" or "all children grow." It's not false, but it's also just a partial truth that doesn't begin to address the problems of teaching and learning. It glosses over the obvious—that children differ enormously in what they can learn, how quickly and easily they learn certain things, and what level of performance they're capable of reaching.

Some children, even with the best teachers, struggle to learn basic reading and math skills by the time they're teens. Others will have mastered reading and/or basic math before they turn five. "All children can learn" is a prime example of a throwaway line, a trivial statement with no real meaning to anyone familiar with real educational problems. Yet there is, as usual, a wee bit of truth to be found in this current champion of slogans that seems to make it irresistible to some.

The shard of truth in a slogan about teaching and learning

It's true that students written off as nonlearners can learn a lot more than their teachers think and can be educated in meaningful and important ways. So I want to be as careful as I can to make myself understood on this point: *We must be careful to discriminate between a teacher's inability to teach a particular skill from that child's ability to learn it. But we must also be careful to discriminate those skills a child can learn from those he can't.* Not all students are capable of learning all things, and there are a few (a miniscule, but probably growing percentage as doctors save ever more severely damaged children) who can learn only the simplest tasks, and then only with extraordinary instructional effort. Some children are permanently unconscious or conscious in some minimal way due to severe physical damage, and while humane care is important, for them "education" seems to be out of the question. Although training them to make a simple response to a particular stimulus might be possible.[3] But, the vast majority of students in special education aren't so severely damaged and can learn a lot when well taught.

If the slogan "all children can learn" is intended as a counterweight to the sentiment "this child can't learn a thing," that's one thing. However, if it's been applied to a child who's fully conscious but difficult to teach, then it's responding to silliness with something even sillier. "All children can learn" is a vapid, misleading statement on two counts. First, it's meaningless unless qualified. Second, if "all" is taken literally to mean each and every child, no exceptions for the permanently unconscious or those with no cerebral cortex, it's patently false. Unless we're talking about learning at the most fundamental behavioral level, like fruit flies that can be trained to make simple responses to specific stimuli.[4]

It's important here to distinguish between training and education. Training might involve no more than eliciting a predictable response to a simple stimulus. For example, you might get responding (like raising an arm) to a simple stimulus (like a buzzer). Or, training might be getting a particular response, like a nod of the head, to a single word like "eat." Education, on the other hand, means learning something relatively complex, like dressing, social interaction, or reading. And when it comes to skills like reading, it's important to distinguish, for example, between the ability to learn to read street signs versus that of reading newspapers. And the difference between just saying the words

that are written and really comprehending them. These distinctions often aren't clear, which results in selling some kids short by including them in instruction that's way too difficult for them.

An especially trite phrase

"All children are special" is a popular variation on this theme, but it's patently silly as well. Sure, all children are genetically unique (identical twins aside) and exhibit a wide variety of characteristics. And all children are or should be special to someone. But the slogan "all children are special" isn't intended to indicate "specialness" in these ways. It's intended to mean that all children are special when it comes to *teaching* them. Every teacher is supposed to see every child as a *special* child, an *exceptional* child in some way, and to *teach* each child like no other child. The slogan is used to argue against seeing only some children as exceptional and therefore in need of a special education. "All children are special" tacitly implies that "all education should be special education." At this unfortunate point, special education becomes tragicomic, as by extension does general education.

The ideas of universal specialness and universal excellence have such appeal as slogans that I fear we may never be able to eliminate them. Reformers seem to bask in the aura of *special* or *excellent* or *elite* but make sure to disassociate themselves from the implications of such words. Specialness and excellence require discrimination in the sense of discernment, the ability to see a significant difference. They require judgment, the recognition that all are not equal in achievement, that some are better than others at some things, that there's a distribution of particular abilities and performances. In America and other nations that hold democratic ideals, we believe that one person shouldn't be judged more worthy than another, *as a person*, and that all people are *equal before the law*. But that doesn't mean that we believe that all people are equal in every which way.

George F. Will has perhaps best captured many experts' unwillingness to make judgments that might reveal an "elite" (a small group that can't, by definition, include everyone; those whose performance or status is extraordinarily high).[5] He notes, for example, that if you designate just about anything as "art" you lose the ability to classify it because nothing is excluded. He suggests that "inclusive" is preferred to "judgmental"—perhaps because inclusive is vague enough to elude any definitive judgment on anything—and he questions whether our democracy is capable of embracing excellence for the very reason that not everyone can be said to have equal "access" to it.

The rhetoric of egalitarianism is so enchanting that it pulls those who should know better under the sludge of irrationality. Maintaining belief in the slogan that *all* children are special when it comes to education perversely ensures its exact opposite, that *no child is seen as special*. Why do we laugh when someone says, "Oh, yes, I'm special, just like everyone else?" Why don't we laugh when someone says, "All children are special?" When we don't laugh, I hope it's because we think it's a bad joke, not because we believe it isn't a joke. Maybe we should just groan. I hope that someday we will laugh people out of positions of public trust for constructing empty, misleading slogans like "all children are special" when it comes to their education.

The meaninglessness of "come to school ready to learn"

The notion that children should come to school ready to learn is triteness multiplied by its tremendous allure. "By the year 2000, every child will enter school ready to learn." This bold statement, hopelessly devoid of any meaning but stuffed full of false promise, was devised by the creators of the "America 2000" education goals in the early 1990s. Obviously, it's a hope that wasn't fulfilled, though embraced by many Republicans and Democrats alike. More importantly, it could never be fulfilled in any meaningful way, regardless of deadline. Changing the date to 2020 or 2200 or any other year wouldn't make any difference. It could well be called dead on arrival with rhetoric that failed to match any conceivable reality. It may have expressed a nice sentiment, but was nothing more than sentimentality gone political. "Ready to learn what, exactly?" we should ask.

It has never been clear to me—or to anyone I've asked about it—just what "ready to learn" should mean. If it means anything, you'd think it would at least mean the child would have acquired skills necessary to receive instruction—like sitting still, paying attention to the teacher, being compliant with requests. It should also mean the child has a high degree of motivation to learn. And it certainly should mean the child has acquired some of the discrimination skills necessary to learn to read—to hear and be able to imitate differences in speech sounds, for example, and associate these sounds with letters of the alphabet. Nor would it hurt if it also means possessing certain basic numeracy skills, such as counting or one-to-one correspondence. We could add numerous other "ready to learn" criteria.

And that's not to count the many variables this slippery slogan fails to consider. For example, there's the matter of the age at which the child enters school. Not all children start school, nor are they ready to start, at the same age.

Ultimately, it doesn't much matter what "ready to learn" means or the age at which the child starts school. There's simply no way to ensure, by any reasonable definition, that every child will come to school ready to learn. Perhaps if we had the resources, we could station a teacher in every home with preschool youngsters to make sure it happened. Or we could forward our own meaningless slogan and arbitrarily say all children are "ready to learn upon arrival," that it's only a matter of "discovering their readiness," which obviously would vary from child to child. But if we do that, why bother setting the goal of all children coming to school ready to learn? They're already ready!

The slogan only has a vestige of sense if "ready to learn" means children were supposed to somehow be different in their readiness by the year 2000. But that's just an arbitrary date that itself has no meaning. Consider the inconvenient fact that neither schools nor any other social agency in our society has the right to *compel* parents to have their children "ready to learn" by the time they enter school, even if we figure out what "ready" means. So even if the slogan could be given some sort of meaning, it would be impossible to achieve its goal. Worse yet, the slogan is an insult to the intelligence of parents of exceptional children. Click and drag this slogan to your trash bin.

This isn't to say it's impossible to encourage families to do a better job of childrearing and nurturing, and to help them learn the basic self-control and paying-attention skills required for successful school performance. We should help more parents teach their children basic phonological awareness (how sounds in words are alike and different), one-to-one correspondence, counting, and a variety of other skills that most successful students have when they enter school. But that's not the same as setting a goal that's both meaningless and impossible.

The dishonesty of "kids don't fail; their teachers fail"

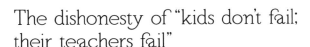

"Kids don't fail, teachers fail" is a familiar indictment used to blame good and bad teachers alike and induce guilt in those whose students are unsuccessful, regardless of the quality of instruction. It's a pity a slogan should be used indiscriminately to accuse many competent teachers who do their best, and who may even offer exceptional instruction. Part of the problem here is the concept of teaching. Part of the problem is also in the recognition that some teachers do without question fail some kids. There's the usual kernel of truth in this catch phrase—perhaps a rather large kernel. But it's not the whole truth. Teachers sometimes fail. Kids sometimes do, too, especially when the goals and the means of achieving those goals are unclear and festooned with gaudy and meaningless slogans.

Teaching and learning are linked, and without learning there is no teaching. That is, a teacher can't use the cop-out, "I taught him, but he just didn't learn!" Anyone who has studied teaching and learning understands how risky it is to allow teachers to use this kind of statement—that they taught, but the kids didn't learn. Teaching can sometimes be very bad, and even mediocre teaching can account for a student's lack of learning. And some teachers blame students for failures that come from their own inadequate instruction. Without exception, teachers should be expected to find and use instructional strategies that are calculated to result in student learning, period.

Nevertheless, every teacher has hit the wall with a kid—done his or her best using the most reliable instructional practices, yet observed little or no progress. While it's true that we have often been too ready to blame children for teachers' faults, the world isn't set right by being too ready to blame teachers for children's failures to learn.

The question remains: can we teach something the student doesn't learn? If so, how do we explain it? If teaching merely means exposing the student to given materials—the teacher's reading, lecturing, or presenting a problem—then the answer is, obviously, *yes*. By that definition of teaching, any child, living or dead, can be taught. By that definition, you can teach a chair just by talking to it! However, if teaching means presenting the student with tasks that result in new skill acquisitions, then the answer is, obviously, *no*. Using this definition, no learning means that no teaching has occurred; the teacher failed. If teaching means using instructional practices known to result

in *most* students' learning the skill in question, then the answer is, obviously, *maybe*.

In the real world, the whole truth is that sometimes people don't respond to the best we have to offer for reasons we don't fully understand. They may be unresponsive to the competent, best efforts of the individual who is trying to help them. Even though their physician gave them the best possible treatment, people sometimes get worse or die. I think it's more than reasonable to assume that a teacher might use the best available instructional practices, yet have a student who learns little or nothing of what she's been trying to teach.

Best practices are those instructional strategies that are usually successful for a particular type of student who's being taught a particular skill. It's necessary to qualify this statement with the type of student and particular skill because students differ dramatically in their prior learning, and skills differ dramatically in their instructional requirements. Many excellent teachers find that they must try multiple approaches to teaching a particular skill to a particular student, even though most of their other students learn the skill with a standard strategy. But many excellent teachers also have fallen short in finding a way to teach some children some skills. Does this mean they've failed? A similar question could be asked of physicians. If a patient doesn't recover from an illness, does that mean the physician has failed? Not necessarily, I think. The fact that something bad happens doesn't mean that somebody was incompetent. Yes, sometimes people do fail. And, yes, sometimes people do just what's recommended by everything we know and still the outcome isn't what we'd hoped for.

I suppose it's human nature to want to blame someone, to have a whipping boy or scapegoat, to hold somebody accountable for what goes wrong. Maybe this is an American predilection, but it's a destructive attitude. Anyone *can* fail, but often we don't know who did or why. Saying that students don't fail, only their teachers, is horribly unfair to teachers (not to mention their students), and if it's taken seriously, it'll drive many good teachers from the profession. True, teachers' organizations sometimes protect bad teachers, just as other professional or labor organizations sometimes protect their incompetent members. That must be recognized and condemned, for it contributes to bad practices and to harming others. But teachers are particularly easy targets for the poison pen and the badmouth, because it's always tempting to look for a facile "solution" to the problem of children or schools that don't meet our expectations.

The false hope of "high expectations"

We hear constantly that we need higher expectations for students. Sometimes, people say we need to have "the same high expectations for all children." But, of course, the same expectations for performance don't fit all students. Getting expectations just right, so that they're not too high or too low for a particular student, is one of the great challenges of being a good teacher.[6] Here's a predictable way for a teacher to screw up royally: have precisely the same expectations for all students.

Of course, we often need to expect more of teachers and schools, too. But seldom do the people who speak of high expectations consider the fact that we should have higher expectations for their thinking! If education were simply a matter of expectations . . . well, I suppose pigs would fly. It's time to say goodbye to the magical thinking that if we just have the right expectations everything's going to be okay.

Columnist William Raspberry has discussed the problem of low expectations in a more reasoned way. To his credit, he doesn't simply blame teachers for having low expectations but indicts others as well: "The critical change . . . is in expectation: on the part of teachers, of course, but also on the part of the rest of us, emphatically including the parents of these children."[7] This doesn't change the fact that if improved performance were simply a matter of increasing expectations—those of teachers or of parents or of both—then improving performance would be a piece of cake. Nearly every teacher, even a very good one who has high but reasonable expectations for students, understands this.

Beware of the promise of the quick and easy fix

Slogans and popular catch phrases often fool people and thereby have dire consequences. They can produce a feeling of self-satisfaction and keep people from doing something that's productive. It's easy to put a bumper sticker or a magnetized ribbon on your car and stop there. It's easy and natural to go along with what teachers or professors or school administrators say and not think things through. Actually doing something to improve schools is harder and takes longer than adopting a slogan.

Too often, we fail to ask just what something means or just how we'd do it or just what evidence supports a popular word or phrase. True, our children often get inferior schooling because of our own tragic

failures. But first, we need to see the humor in the slogans and trite statements that apply to the world of education, have a good laugh, and then get to work fixing it.

Notes for Chapter Four

[1] For more on this phenomenon of myth-making, see Kauffman & Pullen (1996)

[2] Hirsch (1996, pp. 239–240)

[3] Kauffman & Krouse (1981)

[4] Weiner (1999)

[5] Will (2001a); see also Will (2001c)

[6] Kauffman & Landrum (2009a, pp. 414–415)

[7] Raspberry (2001, p. A19)

Part I
Laughing and Crying

Chapter Five:
Thinking Gone Off the Tracks in Other Ways

How Poor Thinking Drove Us Off Track, Creating a Tragicomic Train Wreck of Ideas

Poor thinking abounds. *People suggest things about education that are self-contradictory. Real educational problems are met with denials. Fractured analogies mislead us.* And, as we've already seen, some comments on public education, general and special, are non sequiturs—inferences that don't follow from propositions. Thinking about education can go off the tracks—become irrational—in any of these ways or in any combination of them: self-contradiction, denial, use of the non sequitur, and inappropriate analogy. Real train wrecks are tragic, and ideological train wrecks are too. But *idea-based* train wrecks, typically lacking major tissue damage, also tend to be the stuff of humor. Nonetheless, we need to watch out for the kind of poor thinking I'm going to discuss and to make sure that we don't let it obscure our view of success. And before we get to work fixing the fallout from poor thinking, *we need to pause a moment to laugh at the truly bizarre that it so often inspires.*

Self-contradiction

A seeming contradiction may not actually be one. For example, we might note that a piece of metal is a solid but know that it's made up mostly of space. At an atomic level, all things are mostly space, meaning there's no contradiction in either claim—solid, space. Other times, though, a contradiction truly is a contradiction. For example, we could say that education should be under the control of local authorities, but that we should have a federal law and regulations for schools. In our government, federal regulations supersede state and local regulations, so in the example about education there is truly a contradiction about control—local control, federal control.

Let's consider one particular self-contradiction: that of saying schools should be held accountable for results *and* that at the same time we should have fewer regulations or "strings" attached to schools. This contradiction—accountable, no strings—is blatantly transparent. Deregulation could mean to some people that the sheer number of rules is reduced. So money for schools might be given by the federal government in block grants, and states or localities might be given the freedom to make certain choices of tests to monitor student performance, and so on.

However, "accountability," by its very nature, implies "strings." Replacing a bunch of small strings with a heavier rope is only cosmetic; it isn't actually cutting the strings. The real question is who or what agency has the final say in matters; who can yank your chain. Let's take an example. You could replace a lot of lesser federal regulations on schools with a big one, and if you don't meet federal expectations you might eventually have to close down. It's obvious who calls the tune under these circumstances.

This is essentially what the federal No Child Left Behind (NCLB) law does. The federal rules bind you with serious rope. Suppose the federal expectation is that every school will make adequate yearly progress (AYP) as defined in a federal rule and as demonstrated by standardized test scores. Suppose, furthermore, that a school that doesn't make AYP for three years in a row is considered to be a "failing school" and has to offer parents the choice of sending their child elsewhere. Is this federal or local control of the schools? You bet it's federal control! Deregulation? Not on your life!

I'm thankful for federal control of many things, including the federal special education law. But the law at any level can become silly business. Take NCLB. Another law with a different name but the same requirements would be just as crazy. For example, it can result in a school being labeled as failing because its students with disabilities didn't make the progress demanded by the law on standardized tests or because it missed its AYP for other legitimate reasons. Otherwise, the school would be considered a good or successful school. I ask myself, as I suppose you do, "Is this crazy, or what?"

The fact that some schools and communities see the obvious contradiction in federal demands vs. local control and refuse to go along with the federal law (NCLB) or see it as silly isn't surprising.[1] Federal control of education isn't necessarily a bad thing, but it's important that we see it when it's there. There's no good reason to try to fool people about it by self-contradictory statements.

Denial

A self-contradiction is bad enough, but denial is even more frustrating. Denial takes self-contradiction a step further into never-never land and adds a peculiar fantasy dimension to special education's tragicomedy.

Among the most frustrating denials is the argument that, when it comes down to it, students with disabilities are just like everyone else. How's that for self-contradiction—saying there are students with disabilities, but these students don't actually have disabilities or that we should ignore their differences, which aren't important! We shouldn't see students with disabilities as needing something special because . . . well, so the argument goes, they're not *really* exceptional. They're just students, like all the others, who are different from each other. One line of argument is that we shouldn't see students with disabilities as requiring different treatment; we should treat them just like everyone else. Another suggests there's nothing actually wrong with children who have disabilities except our failure to provide educational environments that match their learning needs. The only problem, then, is our insistence that students with disabilities have problems. They don't have problems; we do.

The denial of these differences we call disabilities has become part of the popular rhetoric about inclusion of students with disabilities in regular classes. This denial is found even among special educators! I admire much of the work of Jim Ysseldyke, Bob Algozzine, and Martha Thurlow. I like them, as I do many of the people whose statements I criticize. But some of their claims puzzle me no end and strike me as the kind of thoughtless prose that helps kill educational programs for students who aren't typical. In one of their books, they say we need to get over seeing some sort of inadequacy or failure of kids with disabilities, and that, "Watered-down curricula, alternative grading practices, special competency standards, and other 'treat-them-differently' practices used with 'special' students must be replaced with school experiences exactly like those used with 'regular' students."[2] Makes me want to scream!

I don't know whether to laugh or cry when I read things like this. But Ysseldyke and his coauthors aren't the only ones to argue that we have to stop seeing students with disabilities as having deficits. Special educators Beth Harry and Janette Klingner also made the argument in their article "Discarding the Deficit Model," published in 2007 in *Educational Leadership*.[3]

These questions bear repeating: There's really nothing wrong with students who have disabilities, except that we treat them differently? They don't actually have deficits? They should be treated like everyone else in school, have the same experiences as those who don't have disabilities—same curriculum, standards, grading . . . ? They set their own goals as they wish, and they either achieve these goals or they don't . . . whatever . . . it's up to them? But, no, Ysseldyke and company weren't writing tongue-in-cheek (or whatever the expression for writing a spoof should be—finger-in-palm, perhaps). Neither were Harry and Klingner. They weren't trying to be funny, like Mark Twain or Garrison Keillor.

In the real world, people with a disability should be recognized as people who do have important abilities, and they should be well-treated in schools as well as in the rest of their lives. But a disability *does* mean a person can't do some particular thing or can do it only with extraordinary difficulty, and some disabilities involve school learning.[4] In plain language, they have deficits. Trying to hide that fact through denial or rhetoric moves us into an imaginary world where things aren't what they seem—only in the fantasy of fiction is this helpful. It doesn't help people with disabilities. It doesn't help society. It doesn't help schools. It only misleads us. And the denial here should be obvious. But some statements aren't so obvious; they're cagey in their denial, but still misleading.

An example is a piece by Dorothy Lipsky and Alan Gartner about special education published in *Harvard Educational Review*. Lipsky and Gartner complain that, "Special education plays a sorting role, both for those consigned to it and for those students who remain in general education."[5]

But, when you stop to think about it, the implication that special education shouldn't "sort" students is seriously misleading. *Of course*, it plays a sorting role! If it didn't, it wouldn't exist, and neither would any program designed for a subpopulation—senior citizens, for example. In fact, special education *must* sort those who need it from those who don't or it becomes an empty practice without point or purpose. Not sorting would mean either that all kids get it whether they need it or not or that kids are just picked for it at random, another kind of sorting that isn't sensible if you're trying to identify only those kids who really need its services. The same is true of any curriculum for any particular group or social program. Really the matter is just this simple: if you have no criteria for participation in the program—if you don't sort—then it can't be special, precisely because it's for everyone.

Any special program has to sort people, whether it's educational, financial, or anything else. Logically, the complaint that it plays a sorting role is a complaint that special education exists! Any educational program that's differentiated has to sort students. That is, it has to include the judgment, "Yes, this one; no, not that one." This is reality for any instructional program, as it is for sports or social security benefits. Even the government has to sort us by age and income history

to give us social security benefits. So, if anything, progress in special education should mean getting better at sorting, the very trait for which Lipsky and Gartner condemn it.

Non sequitur

If self-contradiction, denial, and misleading statements aren't enough, there's always the non sequitur—the seemingly reasonable, all-purpose fooler that combines all kinds of off-track thinking. To create the perfect non sequitur in an argument, you must make sure "then" doesn't issue logically from "if." Here's an example: if the right person doesn't chant at dawn, then the sun won't rise tomorrow. An assumption is made from faulty evidence and thus a fatal disconnect arises, since no one's chant has anything to do with the sunrise.

You don't have to be a keen observer to find non sequiturs in writings from people of all walks of life, including smart people who should know better. It makes me think of two books about postmodernism's foolishness. Alan Sokal and Jean Bricmont in *Fashionable Nonsense* and chapters in Noretta Koertge's edited book, *A House Built on Sand,* show how postmodernists have tried to splice together incompatible grafts of the Heisenberg uncertainty principle (which involves measurement of subatomic particles *only*) onto human affairs.[6] They demonstrate the signature fondness of academics in the arts and humanities for blowsy statements in which premise and inference are supremely unrelated. Educators aren't alone in this folly. Columnist Charles Krauthammer, who holds an M.D. from Harvard Medical School and has practiced psychiatry, made a terrible intellectual booboo in a *Washington Post* column by invoking Heisenberg's principle to explain the uncertainty of the ballot count in the 2000 presidential election.[7] He assumed a nonexistent connection between the election's outcome and Heisenberg's principle. He apparently thought he could fool others, or was himself fooled, into thinking there was a logical connection that didn't in fact exist. Was there uncertainty about the election's outcome? Yes. Was that uncertainty connected in some logical or analogous way to Heisenberg's principle? No.

But, here, our focus is on the use of the non sequitur in arguments about public *education*. For example, Selma Wassermann, a retired professor writing in the *Phi Delta Kappan* education journal, showcases a spellbinding use of the non sequitur by comparing standardized testing to the uncertainty principle in subatomic physics. First, in her argument that educators put too much faith in numbers, she conveniently ignores the fact that Richard Feynman, whom she quotes

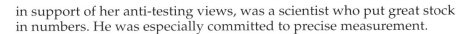

in support of her anti-testing views, was a scientist who put great stock in numbers. He was especially committed to precise measurement.

Wassermann's article reflects a nearly toxic misunderstanding of Feynman's points. For example, she quotes from his essay on values in support of her argument against testing. His argument and hers don't match. She complains that "a new standardized testing movement reappears, with nauseating regularity, every few years"[8] but fails to mention the regularity with which standardized tests have been demonized. Worse, she seems to see quantifying educational performance as both immoral and misleading. Her use of Michael Frayn's play *Copenhagen* to explain Heisenberg's uncertainty principle demonstrates the laughable but all too common misunderstanding of science and measurement. She writes:

> In the play, Heisenberg, the originator of the uncertainty principle, describes its meaning to an audience largely untrained in science: "You can never know everything about the whereabouts of a particle, or anything else . . . because we can't observe it without introducing some new element into the situation—things which have an energy of their own, and which, therefore, have an effect on what they hit." Because of this, he continues, "We have no absolutely determinate situation in the world." Heisenberg's uncertainty principle "shatters the objective universe." The uncertainty principle limits the simultaneous measurement of conjugate variables, such as position and momentum or energy and time. The more precisely you measure one variable, the less precise your measurement of the related variable will be.[9]

First, words attributed above to Heisenberg weren't exactly designed to apply to education. And just because Frayn put words in Heisenberg's mouth doesn't mean they belong there, were ever actually said, or, if they were, that they weren't taken out of context. Most physicists would passionately disagree that Heisenberg's principle means we can't measure *anything* without changing it significantly. Or that it has shattered the objective universe, in which, after all, he plied his trade. The principle of which Heisenberg spoke applies to measuring subatomic particles only; it doesn't apply at all to measuring building materials or student results on standardized testing. To my knowledge, and that of the scientists with whom I've discussed the matter, the Heisenberg principle doesn't even apply to *all* measurement in the *physical* world, and its extension into the field of education is pure nonsense. Consider this statement of Wassermann's: "If quantum theory has any validity, then it should cause us to pause and consider

the kinds of numbers that serve as indicators of student performance on standardized tests."[10] I hope the validity of quantum theory doesn't depend on this analysis and that we don't teach this kind of muddled "thinking" to future generations of our children.

To clarify, physics professor Steve Reynolds of North Carolina State University wrote me about the Heisenberg principle as follows (and I quote with his permission):

The uncertainty principle *does*:

1. Tell us that there are particular pairs of measurable quantities whose values cannot be simultaneously known with infinite precision for a particular object or system (example: east-west position and east-west velocity).

2. Tell us that there are far more possible pairs of measurable quantities that can (at least in principle) be measured with arbitrarily high precision (example: north-south position and east-west velocity).

3. Give us a numerical value for those minimum uncertainties, based on Planck's constant $h = 0.0000000000000000000000000000000066$ 3 joule seconds (6.63×10^{-34} Js).

The uncertainty principle *does not*:

1. Make all measurements uncertain (for example, it doesn't apply to measurements involving discrete counting).

2. Destroy the possibility of objectivity.

3. End experimentation in physics.

4. Have any significant quantitative application whatsoever to objects larger than a single molecule.

5. Cast any doubt at all about the nature of cause and effect.

6. Allow you to ignore other possible practical sources of uncertainty, which are almost always dominant in any real measurement.[11]

Wassermann and others who attempt to apply quantum theory and the uncertainty principle to the macroscopic and social worlds appear to be missing a relatively small but crucial bit of understanding: the scale of

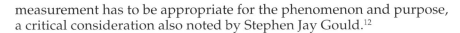

measurement has to be appropriate for the phenomenon and purpose, a critical consideration also noted by Stephen Jay Gould.[12]

Chaos theory, the observation that some mathematical phenomena are not predictable, has captured the interest and imagination of many . . . too many, perhaps. The inexplicably sexy mathematics of chaos are irresistible to some and have thus been "translated" into bizarre and pernicious notions about children and their education, as well as into unworkable ideas about all human interactions. Now, it's true that we can't predict some phenomena over the long term with extreme accuracy. Some phenomena, such as weather, are particularly difficult to predict over long periods, and the mathematics involved demonstrates what has come to be known as "chaos" or "chaos theory." But, does it then follow that chaos is the principle behind everything we fail to understand sufficiently? Probably not. More to the point, if a phenomenon is mathematically chaotic, what does that say about our systematic use of it to solve practical problems? Nothing we want to hear. But that hasn't kept chaos fans from making colorful cognitive leaps and applying its theory to education.

Dr. David Elkind, for example, slaps a postmodern perspective on child behavior disorders by using weather and the dispersion of cream in coffee as examples of chaotic phenomena. And then has the temerity to insist they have crucial implications for teaching difficult children![13] His assumption seems to be that kids, like the weather, are unpredictable. But even if we conclude that the weather is mathematically chaotic, does that give us practical information that applies in a helpful fashion to teaching troubled kids? Or does it do quite the opposite—distract us pointlessly in an intellectually engaging but vain and irrelevant quest for connections to education?

Chaos theory leaves us with nothing but unhelpful trivia. That the dispersion of cream in coffee is chaotic in no way impairs our ability to predict with a high degree of accuracy the color, taste, and caloric value of a given amount of coffee to which a given amount of cream is added. Even against a background of mathematical chaos at some level of measurement, some predications are helpful. Climatology and meteorology give us highly useful short-term warnings. Improved weather predictions are advantageous, allowing individuals to avert risks and harm, even if accurate long-term weather predictions are impossible due to the mathematical chaos of the long-range effects of climatic events.

Some of the silliness about science may come from people's misunderstanding of it when the absurdity gets compounded by attempted applications to education. Most of us believe in a real world governed by reliable laws of physics that are unlikely to ever be overturned. But the real damage to education comes from the idea that social interactions and social development are unpredictable in any meaningful sense. Taken seriously, the idea that we no longer consider human behavior predictable—as related to teaching and managing classroom behavior—leaves teachers unable to develop their craft. Consider some comparisons. Creative and competent musicians hear and use repeated patterns in chords and scales. Without them, they can produce nothing that we recognize as music. Creative, productive mathematicians analyze the regularities in quantitative relationships. Creative linguists find patterns we call grammar. Without finding the predictable relationships, the regularity of patterns, no scientist or artist can make sense of anything. Understanding the predictable patterns in students' behavior is essential to the art and the science of teaching. A master teacher has to be able to see recurrent patterns in students' behavior. That such regularity exists in behavior and that its recognition is essential to teaching is now beyond question.[14] Part of being a competent teacher is being able to see that students' behavior is reasonably predictable.

Among the most obvious non sequiturs in education, as I have suggested, is the use of the Heisenberg uncertainty hypothesis and other borrowings from new physics, or theoretical physics, in which mathematical approximations are proposed to account for the behavior of subatomic particles. Principles of physics are invoked by misguided nonphysicists to suggest dynamic implications for working with children.[15] Likewise, chaos theory and other mathematical phenomena have been "applied" like cheap paint to teaching. The predictable results have instead been chaotic "thinking." Some of these non sequiturs have actually found their way into the professional education literature, adding handsomely to its tragicomedy.

Inappropriate analogy

Argument by analogy has its pitfalls, among them the yawning hole of premises and inferences that are not closely matched, as in the case of the non sequitur. Some analogies are helpful in trying to figure out what education can and can't do, should or shouldn't try, and how education works. But some are just downright inappropriate if you carry them past one match-up of premise and inference.

One of the more enticing ideas is that education should be run like a business. Businesses do make use of reality checks and try to be efficient and effective in their use of resources. Okay so far. But, kids can't be manufactured to uniform tolerances, nor does education have control of its raw materials (students), and so the business analogy rapidly falls apart. Besides, who hasn't run into incompetence, intransigence, waste, fraud, and other frustrating problems in private businesses?

Think it through

Beware that we might not recognize "success" if it jumped up and bit us on our hind parts.[16] Watch out for self-contradictions. Look at denials for what they are. Keep non sequiturs out of education. Don't push analogies too far. Success, like failure, can be hidden by poor thinking or mistaken because of it.

Bottom line, we've got to think things through before we accept an assertion. We'd be wise to think more carefully about what people say and what they propose as "solutions" for education, even if they're "high profile" scholars or perceived as leading authorities. Sometimes, people know what they're talking about; sometimes they don't. And this applies to all of us, including those self-perceived as high and mighty. Self-contradictions, denials, non sequiturs, and fractured analogies are tragic. They're funny, too. Laugh before you cry.

Notes for Chapter Five

[1] See Hahn (2008), Mathews (2008)

[2] Ysseldyke, Algozzine, & Thurlow (2000, p. 67); see also Ysseldyke, Algozzine, & Thurlow (1992, p. 64) for the same statement in an earlier edition

[3] Harry & Klingner (2007); see Kauffman (2009) for commentary

[4] Hallahan, Kauffman, & Pullen (2009), Kauffman & Hallahan (2005a)

[5] Lipsky & Gartner (1996, p. 767)

[6] Sokal & Bricmont (1998), Koertge (1998)

[7] Krauthammer (2000)

[8] Wassermann (2001, p. 32). Humorous misinterpretation of Heisenberg has even found its way into film noir. The defense attorney's strategy in *The Man Who Wasn't There*, a 2001 movie by the Coen brothers, is a black humor send-up of misunderstanding of the uncertainty principle.

[9] Wassermann (2001, p. 35)

[10] Wassermann (2001, p. 35)

[11] Physicist Steve Reynolds provides the following example about how the uncertainty principle could actually be applied to the measurement of a pitched baseball's position, given that we are also measuring its speed: "If the radar gun at a baseball game measures the speed of a pitch to be, say, 91.3 mph, at that instant there is an irreducible uncertainty, according to Heisenberg, in our knowledge of the location of the baseball (along the direction from pitcher to catcher). Let's say the uncertainty [of the radar gun] in the speed measurement is 0.1 mph. For a typical baseball, the corresponding minimum uncertainty in position is about 0.00000000000000000000000000001 inches (10^{-30} in). This is a billion billion times smaller than the radius of a single proton, and is obviously unimaginably smaller than any real uncertainties we would have in measuring the position of anything, even an atom. Similar numbers come out for any macroscopic object. Heisenberg's Principle has ABSOLUTELY NO practical application to macroscopic objects!!!"

[12] Gould (2000)

[13] Elkind (1998)

[14] See Engelmann & Carnine (1982), Kauffman & Brigham (2009), Walker, Ramsey, & Gresham (2004)

[15] For example, Rhodes (1987)

[16] Kauffman (1990, 2008)

Part I
Laughing and Crying

Chapter Six:
The Consequences of Poor Thinking

How the Tragicomic Consequences of Poor Thinking about Education Waste Time and Money and Hurt Children

We must replace poor thinking with critical thinking. As we ponder issues in special and general education we need to ask ourselves questions like the following: Have I heard (or read) this or something like it before? What does this mean? Is this nonsense, or am I just unable to unravel its true meaning? What is a sensible way of looking at this issue or problem? What's going to be the consequence of following through on this idea? Does it use time and money wisely? *If we want good rather than bad consequences for education, we'd better start by using reality-based language that reflects reality-based thinking.*

One of the big favors we can do for each other is communicate effectively so we can make better sense of things and recognize statements and positions that don't add up, no matter who makes them. Too often we fail to apply to education the kind of critical thinking we apply to other problems. Ironically, we often fail to think about problems in public education that require the very skills we want our children to draw on when they're challenged to come up with solutions. The consequences of kids' poor thinking are sometimes amusing, but they can be tragic. *The consequences of adults' poor thinking about public education are often tragicomic, too.* It takes a steely resolution to see the comic side of poor thinking, because the consequences for children and for taxpayers are intensely negative.

Failure of reality checks

A very strange thing happens when people think about education. They don't make use of reality checks, including knowledge of basic science, mathematics, and fundamental statistical concepts, critical thinking, and data. They seem to assume that education operates in an alternate universe where realities don't apply or are safely assumed to be trivial or irrelevant. They seem not to make logical connections between words and what words mean or refer to. They seem not to employ basic concepts, not to demand reliable data, and not to engage in logical inductive or deductive thinking. Yet we rightfully expect school children to do all of these. But somehow, adults' discourse about public education is taken seriously even when their thinking has gone haywire. The result is what one would expect with poor thinking: failure.

And who really pays the tab for nonsense about educating our children? Eventually, all of us who pay taxes for our schools do. We pay more than we otherwise would, and too much of the money we pay is wasted. But our students are those who pay first and most—in wasted time and effort, in miseducation, in lack of opportunity to do what we'd like them to do.

An example of consequences of poor thinking about education

Consider the following story about a child with a real gift that illustrates how popular nonsense about education and reality plays out in schools.

Our 10th grader, Laura, had an interesting assignment: Write a news story about a sequence of events involving a controversial local police action. Her English teacher, Ms. Smith, told everyone in her class to get all the information they could about the incident, then take the perspective of a particular person in the community and write the story from that person's point of view. We thought this would be a really valuable and interesting assignment. It was something Laura really got into.

However, we aren't happy with the way the assignment was handled later in class discussions. We had assumed that Ms. Smith would help students see that different people have different perspectives on what happened or may have distorted the facts, but that she would also help them understand the importance of finding out just what did happen. To our dismay, she took the position that all of the stories were equally valid, equally true. She told Laura that the truth depends on who writes it and that there may be no actual truth to be found. This left Laura rather upset, quite to her credit, in our opinion.

But even more upsetting to her and to us is what happened with other students in the class. According to what we hear from Laura, this kind of thing happens routinely. The school Laura goes to believes that "tracking" is morally wrong and ineffective, so the kids are all in groups of widely mixed ability—"heterogeneous groups," the school people call them. Well, Laura was supposed to discuss her story with her group in some sort of cooperative learning arrangement with three other kids. But, according to Laura, one of the other kids in her group didn't write anything at all and spent the whole time sleeping. Another student wrote a couple of incomprehensible sentences and didn't participate much. The third student in her group wrote a couple of short paragraphs, but she couldn't even read Laura's story.

Laura had read newspaper accounts and even interviewed a couple of people to write her story, which would have filled a couple of newspaper columns. To her credit, she wasn't just upset because she didn't have anybody in her group capable of actually reading and discussing her story. She also was upset because the other students weren't getting anything out of the assignment. Sometimes we think she'd be better off if we just taught her ourselves.

It's hard to know whether to laugh or cry about what happened to Laura. Given the generally poor thinking and low level of discussion about education, it's no surprise to find a conclusion like scholar Roger Shattuck's that "our so-called system of education is far less well-planned and executed than our system of highways and of mail delivery."[1] If we're trying to improve education, whether it's general or special, then we'd better recognize the reality that improvement requires us to take only reality-based comments seriously. Comments not based on reality deserve only laughter and their rejection. Want better use of time and money in education? Want better schools for our kids? Then begin here and now by laughing nonsense out of fashion.

Life is full of absurdities and tragicomedies, but what we say about education shouldn't be among them. When people suggest that all children will be able to perform at a given level above zero, that all children will succeed, or that all students will be proficient, they're contributing to silly talk, not helpful discussion. When people say silly things about education, we should laugh first. We shouldn't take them seriously. Then we should get to work to help people think better about it.

NCLB: a case in point

Some people argue that the No Child Left Behind (NCLB) law at least focuses attention on education's academic outcomes and motivates teachers to work harder to make sure that all of their students, regardless of their personal characteristics, achieve everything they can. But if we respond to silliness in the ways I've been suggesting, then we'll see that NCLB is a prime example of absurd education policy, divorced from data and reality checks. NCLB will probably produce some benefits for some students, maybe even for many students. In fact, just about any policy enacted with good intentions, regardless of how unrealistic it is, will benefit *some* students. Irrational policies like NCLB, however, are doomed to collapse. Unfortunately, in the long term they hurt kids and the cause of education more than they help. And exceptional children are particularly likely to be hurt.

There are several fundamental ways in which NCLB is irrational. One of the things it calls for is "universal proficiency" in math and reading, which is to be achieved by the arbitrary date of 2014. But the very notion of universal proficiency—in fact, the law's focus on a criterion of "proficiency" itself as the measure of educational improvement— is something statisticians find absurd, misleading, and foolish.[2] Statisticians find "universal proficiency" an oxymoron, a contradiction of terms, and a blindness to mathematical realities that would be comical were it not such a serious matter for students and teachers and, ultimately, society.

We have to think about what universal proficiency means—what it means in a down-to-earth, real-world sense. Universal proficiency is indeed an oxymoron—a self-contradiction. So it really doesn't matter whether the target for achieving it is tomorrow or 2014, 100 years or 1,000 years from now. "Proficiency" is defined by assessment of what the majority of individuals can do; universal proficiency is as impossible as having all the children be above average—unless, of course, the criterion for proficiency is set at zero. Perhaps you see the humor in the idea of saying that we're going to achieve universal proficiency, which is as surreal and unrealistic as saying that all human beings will be tall. It's fortunate the law doesn't call for universal proficiency in critical thinking. But, then, that too would be doomed to failure.

Another thing NCLB demands is the elimination of differences in average achievement among various groups, including any distinction between students with and without disabilities. This makes as much sense as waving to the late, blind musician Ray Charles.[3] NCLB makes equal sense (none), because of the defining characteristics of students with disabilities. Even under the federal Individuals with Disabilities Education Act (IDEA), children's disabilities are defined as having a negative effect on school performance. So, we are expected to be dead serious about this idea in NCLB that we can eliminate the achievement gap between children with and without disabilities? Yes, we want under-performing students to do better; no, nonsense is not going to help them do that. We want to end the unfairness of discrimination on the basis of pupils' origin, color, gender, and disability, but irrationality is not the friend of the mistreated.

More nonsense: NCLB also calls for all schools to make what it defines as adequate yearly progress (or AYP). The demand of the law is roughly equivalent to calling for all sports teams to win more games in their league every year than they did the year before, regardless of their

win:loss ratio—and, to make the analogy closer to what is expected of schools, to do this while giving equal playing time in every position to every player on their roster, regardless of ability or training. We see the comedy of applying this idea to our sports teams. Why do we think it's serious when applied to education by our president and Congress and educators and business leaders and journalists? Yet we can just ignore statistical realities when we talk about education? Apparently, some people think so. I don't. I hope you don't, either.

Statistical distributions were totally ignored in a 2007 *Washington Post* editorial.[4] The editorial praised NCLB but stated that the goal of 100 percent proficiency by 2014, "while laudatory, may be unrealistic." No kidding! But, if you're going to say that high standards are great, as the *Post* editorial did, then it's important to realize that higher standards are quite likely to produce more failures, because a standard is set by the percentage of those assessed who can pass it. Every letter to the *Post* about this editorial, including one from the Secretary of Education and the president of the National Education Association, ignored statistical realities. The consequences of the detachment from reality illustrated by these examples are extremely negative—pursuing nonsense, wasting money, misleading the public, and creating false hopes, to name a few.

NCLB and many comments about it are unhelpful in calling for impossible outcomes. In fact, any public policy (law) and any commentary that calls for the impossible is unhelpful, to say the least. Tragicomic is more like it. NCLB makes a mockery of critical thinking. It is, in fact, an example of very poor thinking. It's as childish as would be a law requiring the National Aeronautics and Space Administration (NASA) to change the speed of light, invent an anti-gravity device, or build a perpetual motion machine. Childish policies waste time, effort, and money that could be spent on things that make sense. But then, the kind of truth we're after isn't made by one's declaration of the desire to make something happen. Truthiness, however . . . that's another matter.

Most people understand how stuff created in the physical sciences is doomed to failure when it disregards or is ignorant of reality. For example, people aren't allowed to construct and sell airplanes if they've ignored gravity or aerodynamics. Talk about any kind of education that doesn't recognize important realities, like statistical distributions, shouldn't be accepted either. Talk that ignores realities should be rejected simply because any proposal for reform, legislation, or regulation that doesn't start with the idea that realities have to be dealt with is sure to fail. Ideas that ignore reality might appeal to a lot of voters, might be sold to unsuspecting people, and might seem at first to be successful. But ultimately they crash and burn, just as they do in the natural sciences when reality is ignored. NCLB is a case in point of an education policy that's ultimately doomed to failure because it ignores realities. It's decidedly not even logical or reality-based, much less evidence-based.[5] What a waste!

Other ways of ignoring reality

Unfortunately, NCLB isn't the only poorly thought-out education policy. It's just a convenient example of a law that many people know about. Ridiculous statements about special and general education and the policies designed to match them are common but incompatible with education's goals. I've said before, "Especially in the case of education, which at its most fundamental level is helping people make sense of things, senseless rhetoric runs against the grain of what one is trying to accomplish."[6] Still, "senseless rhetoric" describes a lot of what has been written and said about education. How do we account for this? It's enough to make you laugh and then want to cry about what it does to children and their teachers, parents, communities, and the nation.

Most people realize that when they ignore reality they are risking tragedy. In fact, when someone ignores reality we usually say they're mentally ill, or at least doing something very dangerous. We try to teach our students and our own kids about realities so they don't hurt themselves or others. If they ignore a reality, we restrict and warn them about the dangers of assuming reality doesn't apply to them. We want our students and our offspring to talk and act as if they live in a real world in which some things are always, unalterably true, regardless of anybody else's arguments or wishes to the contrary.

Regrettably, many people who talk about education and its improvement seem to assume that realities are trivial. They are working from a false premise. Sometimes, the premise is based on the philosophy that realities are just social conventions, just cultural biases, just ideas of the powerful foisted on the oppressed, not universal truths. Or they might assume that the truth is made simply by consensus. If you don't buy this, just read up on postmodernism or check into the notion of "truthiness" or "wikiality." Sometimes, the false premise shows ignorance or misunderstanding. Or, it might show political finesse in spite of its irrationality. Sometimes it's expressed as a desire to "think outside the box," as if the "box" of realities is an artificial constraint on creativity. Sometimes I think it shows extreme frustration with education policy. People may know that the policy (NCLB, for example) is unrealistic, but they support it anyway because

they believe it's the best we can hope for. Or they might say that at least it's a step in the right direction.

Still, regardless of *why* anyone thinks and talks as if realities don't exist in education, or that data can be interpreted willy-nilly, the consequences are very, very negative. You have to wonder what some would say of a new cancer treatment that has cured 10 percent of its recipients but killed or worsened the other 90 percent. Would they say, "Well, at least it's a step in the right direction; we've got to put this on the market!"? In some areas of our lives, we use rational judgment fairly well. Why don't we "get it" that we have to be rational about public education to avoid tragic mistakes?

Education and complicated realities

There's the old, familiar saw about relatively simple things, "Well, it isn't rocket science." In a lot of ways, education—especially special education—*is* rocket science. It's complex, difficult to understand, and disastrous when we ignore even a single, fundamental reality. Space shuttle tragedies occurred because such seemingly small realities were overlooked. As with space flight, getting most things right but being wrong in one critical way has resulted in tragedies. Nor is getting things mostly right about education good enough. In public education, we too often forget or ignore realities some see as inconvenient or trivial but that result in predictable, inevitable failure.

There are going to be those who believe that we should return to the "good old days" of education, as if we could somehow return to what they think was a much less complicated world. We could argue ad nauseam about how complicated lives were a century or more ago compared to today. The reality is, though, we can't go back. Even if things weren't so complicated then, they are now. What do we want, schools that prepare kids for life in 1850? 1950? Even if you make the assumption that teaching wasn't rocket science in the old days (I think it was, but people just didn't know it), it is today.

Regardless, one reasonable expectation is that education should help students separate fact from fiction and deal rationally with our confusing world. If we teach that fact can't be distinguished from fiction, we'll always have a problem. We'll have big problems as long as our talk of public education doesn't forthrightly acknowledge complicated realities and reject as frivolous the fictions and simple answers to which people cling. When we talk nonsense about education or accept silly ideas as reasonable, our children fail to learn the importance of rational thinking. This consequence is bad enough for general education, but profoundly so for special education.

Burying kids in intellectual trash while wasting time and money

It's bad enough that poor thinking about education wastes massive amounts of taxpayer money and that it creates frustration and anger among adults who care about schools. But it's nearly criminal, in my opinion, that kids get buried in the rubble. In addition, the discussion of education and its reform reduces students to abstractions. The kids become subjects in the worst sense of the word, just youngsters about whom we spin our "theories," for or about whom we write scripts or narratives but never confront as flesh and blood or as individuals like ourselves. Yet their needs remain the same: these are kids who need skills, knowledge, encouragement, and success.

It's much easier to pretend that kids don't really need to be taught particular things, that whatever "knowledge" they construct for themselves is fine and that their lives will be improved by our mantras or whatever mumbo-jumbo we feel good about. The abrogation of our responsibility is easy, especially when we provide cover for it by talking and writing nonsense. The nonsense doesn't help the kids. It does help those who acquiesce or promote it. They may gain status, security, and power in certain quarters, particularly in higher education and in political contests.

Failure to challenge poor thinking

Many contemporary Americans seem to consider it rancorous—bad form, mean-spirited, ill-tempered, offensive—to question the meaning of a statement directly. Unfortunately, many people in higher education seem to think that's true too. In higher education, "we find professional unwillingness to be seen to criticize colleagues in the guild."[7] In politics, the public is fed statements by candidates that often go unchallenged. Candidates for public office don't usually exchange and challenge each other's statements in any depth in debates. Debate moderators and those who interview candidates seldom follow any systematic line of questioning to get at the meaning of a proposal. If they do, they are said to be arrogant or rancorous, or to be appealing to "elite" voters.

Not challenging a statement that doesn't make sense or that contradicts a previous statement can be taken as a sign of respect. In fact, the

moderators and interviewers of candidates for public office often focus on trivialities. There seems to be an anti-intellectual bias among a significant proportion of the public, an assumption that someone of average intellectual capacity in a position of public trust should be preferred to someone who is highly intelligent. A more dangerous assumption is that most people will see a silly question or an empty answer for what it is. Assuming that people will recognize a silly or empty answer doesn't improve public discourse about education or anything else.

Although I've used NCLB as an example of nonsensical public policy, the problem of poor thinking and its unpleasant progeny isn't peculiar to the political left or right. *Boston Globe* columnist Thomas Oliphant suggested that President George W. Bush's political organization appears to have taken the "leave no child behind" slogan from Marian Wright Edelman's Children's Defense Fund.[8] That the slogan originated with Edelman's or Bush's organization . . . doesn't matter a bit. It remains meaningless rhetoric in NCLB regardless of its origin.

Oliphant suggests that Edelman and the Children's Defense Fund would like to achieve higher incomes, improved health care, and better housing for poor children. Almost everyone would like to achieve those things, and with appropriate language these objectives are reachable. "Leaving no child behind" isn't even possible, unless "behind" doesn't really mean behind in NCLB. If Edelman used "behind" as a figure of speech meaning "forgotten" or "neglected," that makes sense. Raising incomes, improving health care, and improving housing are all real-world, achievable goals. The following, however, are not: that no one person has the lowest income, the poorest health care, or the most humble abode. Nor can we boast that nobody will have lower incomes, poorer health care, or more humble housing than the average. Bottom line: we can't create a perfectly equal and average lifestyle for everyone. Failure to come to grips with this reality will produce tragedy sooner or later. Yes, we can reduce disparities between privileged and underprivileged—but only to a point, even in material things, and only then if we're willing to give up unfettered freedom to pursue wealth. And when it comes to intellectual disparities, the "no child left behind" idea in the NCLB sense is pure poison.

We try to teach children to take on tasks that can be accomplished, to challenge themselves with *solvable* puzzles, to separate the possible from the impossible. We want them to recognize exaggeration. So why do public officials make statements that, coming from children, we'd feel compelled to correct? High aspirations, yes; sophistry or quixotry, no. We don't want children to aspire to trisecting an angle, to eliminating the gap between 5 and 6, or to finding the real place in which all the students are above average. Then, why do we allow people to aspire to achieve equally silly things in public schooling?

Ask good questions to avoid bad consequences

Education may fail for reasons other than poor thinking, but poor thinking ensures its failure. Those who propose public policies too often fail to ask necessary questions: Can we actually do this? How will it work? Will it work for long? How is it better? Will we run into the same problems again? So much of the disappointment with reform is highly predictable that many astute observers have wondered why more good thinking isn't found among the brightest among us, including captains of business and people in institutions of higher education who say ridiculous things.[9] If *they* don't ask these good questions, we must.

The reality is that people are smart about particular things; they can be extraordinarily bright and capable and reality-based about some things, yet extraordinarily naive about something else, about which they say things that just don't compute. Part of the problem for all of us as citizens is recognizing this and being able to tell the difference between the reasonable and the preposterous when solving a *particular* problem. One of our biggest problems is doing as adults what we ask kids to do—think about things carefully, not make snap judgments, not assume a popular trend is necessarily good, or something unpopular is necessarily bad, and always ask ourselves, "Let's see, how would this work out?" We don't like it when kids make obvious logical errors in their thinking because we know that these ideas will lead to disappointment. We shouldn't tolerate poor thinking about public education, special or general. Poor thinking, which we can infer from language, makes a mess of things and results in foolish behavior and tragicomedy.

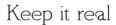

Keep it real

If our schools are *not* to be tragicomic, then we need to keep our language about them tied to realities. The consequence of unreal language is messed up schools. Ignoring reality wastes time and money that could be used for improving schools. The waste is bad enough in itself. It hurts us. Even worse, it hurts our kids. Let's start by understanding the tragedy of it and seeing its comic twist.

By the way, we could even invent a slogan about education that makes sense: "every child well taught." Four words, same as "no child left behind." Applies to special education, too. Teaching every child well would be difficult, but at least within the realm of the possible. We could take the slogan literally. It would still be a slogan. But because it's closer to the real world, it's a slogan with fewer negative consequences.

Notes for Chapter Six

[1] Shattuck (1999, p. 34)

[2] Betebenner (2008), Ho (2008), Rothstein, Jacobsen, & Wilder (2006)

[3] Kauffman (2005)

[4] *Washington Post* (2007)

[5] Kauffman & Konold (2007), Konold & Kauffman (2009)

[6] Kauffman (2002, p. 284)

[7] Conquest (2000, p. 223)

[8] Oliphant (2001)

[9] For example, Lloyd & Hallahan (2007), Rothstein et al. (2006), Sarason (1990), Sasso (2001), Tanner (2000)

Part II
Thinking and Fixing

Containing six expository chapters on:

1. How improved understanding of the role of schools in our society can lead to more rational decisions

2. How better thinking about tests can help us improve our understanding of schools

3. How rational thinking about direct instruction can make schools more effective

4. How we can group students most effectively for instruction

5. How better judgment about successful schools can spur on improvement

6. How we can better advise policy makers about education

Chapter Seven:
The Role of Schools in Our Society

How Improved Understanding of the Role of Schools in Our Society Can Lead to More Rational Decisions

As we saw in Part I, the nonsensical treatment of education comes from many sources. And all that nonsense contributes to the tragicomedy that public education has become. Much of the popular reform rhetoric at both ends of the political spectrum, extreme right and left, is vapid almost beyond belief and adds to the tragicomedy. Awareness of this intellectual folly begs the following question: in this atmosphere, how do we go about making sense of things in education? We now need to ask, "What can we do about it?" Remember that, as Mark Twain knew, laughing at absurdity is the *only* effective tool we have in fighting this ripening heap of rubbish. A major part of it is expecting schools to do everything. We need to understand this: *schools have to be first and foremost about instruction that produces academic competence*. If they aren't, then they deserve to be thrown away. Sure, they can and should do some other things, too. But they can't do everything. And this point stands: *if they don't produce academic competence to the greatest extent possible, then they aren't good*. If we can't do this, success in other areas is almost irrelevant.

School boards, schools, and students: all implicated in the tragicomedy

School boards have come under a lot of humorous criticism about education. For example, in *Following the Equator*, Mark Twain wrote, "In the first place God made idiots. This was for practice. Then He made School Boards."[1] School boards often are said to have made silly, blatantly irrational decisions. In truth, sometimes they have done so. But, it's ultimately the citizens of a district who're responsible for the election of public officials who control schools and establish education policy, even in the case of appointed boards. This allows each district to represent itself in accordance with its nature as a community. Among other reasons, we choose where we live in large part because of this community nature. So for better or worse, this responsibility is placed squarely in our hands. Yet it's adults, including educators but others as well, who have the upper hand in making public education tragicomic. If tragicomedy is the object of the game, they might be considered to have played their hand well; if effective education is the object, they have played it poorly. Truthfully, we only have ourselves to blame.

Besides the adults who make education policy, students have their own way of adding to the tragicomedy. Mark Twain recalls that a fifteen-year-old girl reported to a crowd of his schoolmates, "Here is a boy seven years old who can't chaw tobacco."[2] He was humiliated, as students still are today, by taunts from classmates for his failure to conform to peer expectations. Mark Twain noted:

> By the looks and comments which this [girl's comment] produced I realized that I was a degraded object; I was cruelly ashamed of myself. I determined to reform. But I only made myself sick; I was not able to learn to chew tobacco. I learned to smoke fairly well but that did not conciliate anybody and I remained a poor thing and characterless. I longed to be respected but I never was able to rise. Children have but little charity for one another's defects.[3]

An important insight is that American public schools and special education in particular have *always* been considered tragicomic by at least some writers. Schools have always been changing in one way or another, and some people have considered the changes good while others see them as unfortunate. For example, in his 1864 send-up of the schools of his day entitled "Miss Clapp's School," Mark Twain commented, "They sing in school, now-a-days, which is an improvement upon the ancient regime; and they don't catch flies and throw spit-balls at the teacher, as they used to do in my time—which is another improvement, in a general way."[4] So, are we to assume that singing is good—a part of arts education? Or was Mark Twain being sarcastic? One might interpret him either way. And what of throwing spit-balls at the teacher? Was he defending or condemning misbehavior? And does it matter? A certain degree of calculated cynicism in regards to just about everything is a healthy all-American attribute. It makes us laugh.

What should schools do? Old questions

Just what should schools do, and what is *not* their business? For what should teachers be held accountable, and for what should they *not* be responsible? Do schools shape society, or does society shape schools? How has the role of schools in our society changed since we were elementary school students? These are questions as old as public education. They are also difficult but important questions, and we could pose many more queries about the role of schools in American society today. Some of our peers may find our answers insufficient or laughable, either because we omit something they believe is important for schools to do or because they're convinced schools shouldn't even try to do what we think they must.

For example, for which students should public schools be held responsible? The answer, again, has changed over time. A century ago, the majority view was that a lot of children with disabilities didn't belong in regular public schools. That changed in significant ways in the public mind when educating children with disabilities became a legal mandate in 1975 with the passage of the first federal special education law, then known as the Education of All Handicapped Children Act, and now known as the Individuals with Disabilities Education Improvement Act (often simply called IDEA). Nowadays, the legal view and the view of most Americans is that *all* exceptional children are to be educated at public expense and that the vast majority of these children belong in regular public schools.

But, the education of exceptional children must be seen in the context of what schools are for. Historically, politicians and philosophers have suggested at one time or another that schools should do the following by the time a student graduates from high school:

Ensure that students are competent in basic academic skills

Prepare students for employment

Prepare students for further education, especially college

Prepare students to be good citizens in a democracy

Prepare students for independence as adults

Prepare students to pass on or perpetuate American culture

Prepare students to live successfully in a multicultural society

Ensure that students are equipped to achieve self-fulfillment

Equalize opportunities for all citizens.

Some of these are overlapping roles. More roles or expectations could be added or stated in slightly different ways, but the main idea in all cases is that schools should be getting children ready to be competent, successful adults in our society. In all cases, too, we could ask for clarification. For example:

What is academic competence?

What are basic academic skills?

How do we judge that an adolescent or young adult is ready for employment?

What is self-fulfillment?

How is independence demonstrated?

How do we know that education is multicultural?

How do we know when opportunities have been equal?

Getting really specific about just what schools should accomplish is more difficult than it seems. And, of course, individuals have always had very different ideas about what public schools should do, so getting a majority opinion or consensus about the role of schools is important. The role of public schools ultimately depends on what most of the people who control them think. It has always depended on what they think schools should be expected to do and how much money should be spent to accomplish those goals.

Education's history: the legacy of the role of schools

The history of education can be traced back thousands of years. Its American version started with European notions of what schools are for and what they should provide for students and society. My purpose here is to outline the various functions of schools in *American* culture since the beginning of the New Republic. Because I was for more than three decades a professor of education at the University of Virginia, which Thomas Jefferson founded, I'm aware of many of the things our third president said about the importance of public education. One was, "If a nation expects to be ignorant and free, in a state of civilization, it expects what never was and never will be."[5] As my friend and colleague, education historian Jennings L. Wagoner, has noted, Jefferson was intent on promoting the public education of rich and poor alike. But his view of education has undergone considerable

elaboration and change. Over the centuries of American public education, we have seen various emphases, such as the following:

Basic education in literacy and numeracy

Citizenship education

Character or moral education

Religious education

Vocational or industrial education

College preparatory education

Arts education

Social education or socialization

Multicultural education

Physical education

Gifted education

Special education for students with disabilities

Schools as centers for all services to children

These are not the only emphases that could be listed, but they're among those most people will recognize immediately as part of American public schooling. Throughout the years, some roles have been emphasized more than others, and in nearly every era of American history, prominent citizens have criticized public schools for including or neglecting one or more of them.[6]

When the American democracy was established, the founding fathers saw the need for an educated populace—citizens who could read and do basic arithmetic—to maintain the government of the republic. In the early decades of the new nation, from its founding in the late eighteenth century to the mid-nineteenth century when public schools became common, the focus was on basic academic skills: reading, writing, and arithmetic. The agrarian calendar was followed (that is, schools operated primarily during the winter months, and weren't in session during the time of peak farm activity when youngsters were needed to help at home). This idea of the school calendar, with summer months free, has been maintained for nearly two centuries. It's been hard to change, though alternative school calendars may eventually catch up with America's urbanization and the realization that even in rural areas in the twenty-first century children aren't usually needed for farm work.

A focus on the basic academic skills of literacy and numeracy—words and numbers—remains controversial. Likewise, the idea of rote memory of information, often attacked today as the focus for passing tests, remains a matter of argument. Don't be fooled into thinking that the distaste for memorization and rote repetition is a recent development. Mark Twain and Charles Warner collaborated in writing the 1874 novel *The Gilded Age*, in which they said:

> The children were put to school; at least it was what passed for a school in those days: a place where tender young humanity devoted itself for eight or ten hours a day to learning incomprehensible rubbish by heart out of books and reciting it by rote, like parrots; so that a finished education consisted simply of a permanent headache and the ability to read without stopping to spell the words or take breath.[7]

Oh, yes, it seems we've always considered some of the things taught in schools "incomprehensible rubbish" and noted the folly of training kids to repeat it like parrots. But we've also gone through periods of considering nothing at all to be essential knowledge and of expecting kids to memorize nothing whatsoever. It's very hard for us as a society to recognize that the forceful rejection of one extreme can lead to the silliness of the opposite extreme.

Controversies: what, how, and level of learning

Controversies about education have always swirled around three major issues: first, *what* children should learn (what they should study, sometimes called the school *curriculum*); second, just *how* they should be taught the things they should learn (also known as *instruction*); and third, the *level* at which they should learn facts, be able to deal with ideas, or be able to perform tasks (the issue of *standards* of learning). In the 1980s, there was considerable debate about cultural literacy, or what all American schoolchildren should study.[8] School reformers have for more than a century debated about standards for students and teachers and argued about the best instructional methods.[9] Unfortunately, the most reliable data and careful, rational thinking have been less influential than philosophical posturing and political maneuvering

in affecting educational policies.[10] And, sadly, this remains true in contemporary American education, including the No Child Left Behind Act.[11]

Returning to the flow of history, by the late nineteenth century, American schools were not just one-room, multi-age affairs in rural areas but included large schools in urban areas with students grouped according to age or grade. Moreover, many immigrants came to the nation, a trend that continued well into the twentieth century and is with us in the twenty-first. So school systems in many parts of America have had to contend with urbanization and immigration in addition to industrialization and deindustrialization. Little wonder that nineteenth-century American education set the stage for philosophical arguments that have lasted more than 100 years.[12] As never before, vocational education, multicultural issues, education in the arts, and special programs for the most highly gifted students and those with disabilities became controversies in the nineteenth century. These are all issues that excite us still today.

The world wars, particularly World War II, caused Americans to think more seriously about how education functions in a democracy and how it should prepare all citizens for participation in society.[13] The need for literate soldiers pointed to the necessity of schools that teach basic literacy and numeracy. The wars also highlighted the necessity of vocational skills that make America competitive. The war effort and the return of soldiers to employment and other social roles reminded people that the nation needs its best and brightest but can ill afford the loss of its citizens with disabilities. Consequently, special education for students at both ends of the ability spectrum got a significant boost in the minds of those who determine school policy. Especially with the GI bill, college preparation became a matter of great importance for high schools.

Beginning midpoint of the twentieth century, the racial desegregation of public schools and the civil rights movement made people think again about the need for multicultural education and equalizing educational opportunities for all identifiable groups. And new waves of immigration in the twenty-first century compel further thought on how to accommodate cultural diversity in schools. Multicultural education requires understanding one's own culture and others' and the part education plays in a social context. Critics of multicultural education, as well as some supporters, paint it as a rejection of "universal" standards of learning and instruction. They're worried that it sets up a situation in which the school must have very different expectations and instruction for students specific to their parentage and cultural background. The fact that the literature on education simply doesn't support "culturally sensitive" instruction as it is typically portrayed (that students need different types of instruction depending on cultural identification or "learning style") doesn't keep people from embracing such misleading notions as learning styles and other scientifically groundless ideas.[14]

The late twentieth and early twenty-first centuries have been an era of rapidly growing technologies, particularly in information processing and communication. Electronic networks, including the World Wide Web, have changed much about how information is accessed, stored, conveyed, exchanged, and processed. The technological developments in communication have not only enhanced the accessibility of reliable information but elevated the ability to misinform. Image and fact, truth and lie, fact and speculation are increasingly difficult to identify, especially for children lacking clear guidance and for gullible adults. Little wonder that the sophistry of postmodernism, which depends on the assumption that the truth about nothing can be established, should become popular in this intellectual climate. Understandably, in an era in which postmodernists suggest that truth itself is a myth and science a trivial pursuit, the characteristics of effective teachers are said to be only matters of opinion. The implications of this kind of thinking for education, whether special or general, are . . . well, so negative as to be almost unthinkable.

What we want in teachers

The characteristics, education, training, and employment of teachers have always been issues of great importance in schools, both for those working in institutions or engaged as instructors of special groups of students and for those teaching in typical schools or what might be termed "general education."[15] The training of teachers is often poo-pooed as fluff, the trivial stuff of teaching methods, whereas knowledge of subject matter is assumed to be sufficient to make a teacher competent. However, many individuals who are quite knowledgeable and experienced in their subject matter (say, math or chemistry or literature) are failures as teachers because they don't know how to manage the behavior of their students or because they know little about imparting their knowledge. Teacher education has been wrecked in large measure, not only by "educationists" who insist on failed methodologies but by well-meaning academics and social critics outside of education who peddle nonsense about teaching and

learning.[16] After all, if your assumption is that science is outmoded and all truth is a mirage, is it any wonder that you've wrecked teacher education?[17]

The school reform theme

"School reform" has been a theme played (terribly out of tune) by politicians for a very long time.[18] The early twenty-first century is no exception; the George W. Bush No Child Left Behind (NCLB) initiative is but a contemporary version of reform efforts that go back many decades. The concern for uniform testing, higher standards of learning or exit criteria, greater rigor in the classroom, closing gaps between various groups, and higher expectations for teachers and pupils have very long historical roots.

Why do these reform issues get repeated over and over like bad pop tunes? Maybe it's because we want certain values like democracy and high expectations to stay with us, so we want our schools to teach democratic values and make kids work hard and achieve everything they can. That's not a bad tune. But at the same time, we may worry that schools just keep too many things the way they are, like differences in social class (kids go to college because their parents did and they're expected to; students whose parents are working class go into vocational training and get jobs right after high school because they're not considered college material by the schools). Here we have what might be considered a different tune or a tune in a different key. These themes sewn together make nothing but dissonance.

So which changes first, our schools or our social values? And should schools change society, or should society change schools? The reality is that society and its schools exert reciprocal influence on each other. Historian Dickson Mungazi said, "In many respects education is the process of adjusting to social values in the same way education defines social values. It is highly sensitive to the operative social norms. Any change in society and the values of society itself must be reflected in the educational process."[19] Maybe every generation has to figure this out, so out-of-tune school reform themes or melodies that don't mesh get played over and over until reform movements kick in with solutions. In the meantime, it's enough to make you want the sweet sounds of silence.

Maybe we'd hear a better-tuned reform theme if we could agree in understanding that the central role of schools—their priority—is *making children competent in the academic arena.* That is, after all, their fundamental purpose. That theme leads to sensible public education policies. If it's taken seriously, that understanding should lead to a coherent focus on instruction in academic skills and on the insistence that teachers use the instructional methods that have the strongest basis in carefully designed field tests. We want our children to learn many things, but the priority of the schools is to teach academic skills to all who can learn them. Now that is one lovely, lilting tune, while the other things schools do, though important, are secondary to academic instruction.

Nonacademic self-care skills—that can only be taught in designated, discreet areas or would otherwise be embarrassing for those who need them—are critically important for students who struggle mightily to learn even the most basic academic skills. Focusing on students' presence in the general education classroom at the expense of learning these critical skills is a tragicomic breach of public trust. It creates excruciating dissonance. Think heavy metal at its worst. True, there are many things besides academics that we want our children to learn. And it's not true that *all* students can learn academics, particularly at the same "high" level. Nevertheless, we do want all students who can do so to reach a high level of academic achievement. We do want our kids to do better than they have academically. And if our society insists that our schools make academics their priority, our schools will produce students better equipped to perpetuate the values of democracy and high expectations and care for those less fortunate.

Accountability

It's tempting to conclude that our public schools are responsible for everything, or conversely, nothing. That is, nearly everything is included in today's public school mission (to meet all the needs of all the wildly diverse children who attend them), but we hear constant complaints that schools are too seldom held accountable. Accountable for what? How? Some supposedly contemporary ideas put the schools at the center of all kinds of services to children and their families. However, in the now distant past of the 1960s, psychologists/special educators Esther Rothman and Pearl Berkowitz proposed a "clinical school" in which one could find (1) a citizens group program, (2) a law program, (3) a dental-medical program, (4) a teaching program, (5) a therapy program, (6) a welfare program, (7) a research program, and (8) a professional training program.[20] Clearly, making schools the center of all kinds of child services is not a novel idea today. But neither is the idea that schools should be held accountable primarily for children's academic learning.

For exactly what should schools be held accountable? For test performance alone? For teaching the "whole child?" For teaching children according to their learning styles and teaching them about global cultures? For including all students in their regular or typical classes, no matter the student's learning history, abilities, or other characteristics? For making all children feel welcome and valued? For teaching students study habits, morals, personal responsibility, civic responsibility?

These are not trivial questions, especially for teachers and school administrators. And an often-heard idea is that schools should practice "wrap-around," meaning that the schools should be accountable for "wrapping" *all* of the services a student might need around the student in school (much like the Rothman/Berkowitz idea of the 1960s, but maybe even more than their eight kinds of services). But without a clear focus on teaching academics, I'm afraid the schools are in danger of self-suffocation from all that wrapping.

The primacy of academic competence

In my opinion, what Siegfried Engelmann wrote about the role of schools in the 1960s remains true today.[21] His take was that schools must focus on helping children gain academic competence. He warned that educators must not see themselves as policy makers but as instruction experts. He wrote, "They cannot make up objectives that are inconsistent with society's general commitment to make children competent in the academic arena."[22] True, many people want schools to do many, many things. Many things they are incapable of doing beyond the role of making children competent in academics. But if schools fail in their academic role—in helping students make progress toward or in achieving academic competence—then they are truly derelict. Most children with disabilities can gain basic academic competence, although some of them are not going to reach this goal at the same time as their age peers. And for a few children with disabilities, competence in basic self-care skills, rather than academic competence, needs to be the goal and is critically important to their lives. Academic competence isn't for everyone, but if schools don't teach academic skills to all who can learn them, then the students who need something other than a focus on academics aren't likely to be well served either.

Multiculturalism in its best sense is entirely consistent with schools' focus on academic competence. We do need teachers who understand and respect each student's cultural heritage and community. And teachers must understand that students have a right to keep their native language and culture. We need teachers who are sensitive to individual students *and* competent in instructing them in the skills they'll need for future opportunities.[23] If they're not competent in academic instruction, then they really can't be sensitive in ways they should be to students' cultures. As far as we can determine, all individuals learn in basically the same way, and no excuse for not teaching students the skills they need is acceptable. Students don't fail to learn academics because of who their ancestors are. The degree to which parents want or don't want their kids to learn to read and communicate and understand mathematics, and all the things we associate with academic competence, doesn't depend on where they came from. When it's what it should be, multiculturalism is a way of ensuring that all students learn all the academic skills they can and have equal opportunities for all of life's good things, regardless of their parentage or life circumstances. To that limited degree, an appropriate and robust academic education trumps parentage and culture.

The seduction of image

In the early twenty-first century, the image presented by schools is thought by many to be the critical feature of their role. The image is enhanced by test performance but includes much more. Writer Milan Kundera warned of what he called "imagology," which is the gradual replacement of idea by image.[24] He worried that image would become the measure of truth. Nowadays, schools must project an image of high performance, but in addition they are expected to present an image of inclusiveness, comprehensiveness, and instruction in social rectitude. The presence of many immigrant families, the wide divergence of economic resources of families and communities, concern about students' use of recreational drugs and their participation in violence or bullying, and placement of many students with disabilities in general education classrooms all contribute to the anxiety of teachers and administrators about meeting the expectations of the public, about presenting a public image of "can and will succeed brilliantly at whatever task is given us, no excuses, no extra cost."

Some schools knuckle under to the image of meeting the unintelligent, unrealistic requirements of NCLB (as I noted in earlier chapters, NCLB ignores important realities about statistical distributions, resulting in silly expectations). Others develop an image that is at least equally as cockeyed as NCLB but opposed to NCLB expectations. The image they project is that they really care about students as human beings but don't care much, if at all, about their test performance. They

work on their image as egalitarian, welcoming institutions in which "differentiated instruction" means that all children's instructional needs are met in heterogeneous groups.

But when image becomes more important than substance, schools fail in their mission to make children competent in the academic arena. For example, schools that unilaterally place all students in general education regardless of what students can do or that group children in certain classes without regard to their abilities may pass the popular test of image. They may be described as "inclusive," yet fail the students by not teaching them all they can. Similarly, schools may adopt popular reading programs that are based on literacy and exploration of books but exclude or minimize the foundational skill components of reading. The foundational skills may look mundane and unattractive to the untrained eye, but the programs that neglect them typically fail, and fail substantively, because most students don't learn to read or do arithmetic or otherwise perform as expected.

Even institutions of higher education aren't shielded from the battle of style vs. substance. The proclivity of teacher training programs to focus on teaching a diversity of skills to diverse populations instead of effective instruction in foundational skills results in a workforce that is unable to evaluate teaching critically. If we tell teachers that they should accommodate *all* of the diversity of students at multiple levels of learning ability, then we miseducate them; we teach them something that isn't true, just truthy. And when we do this, we don't just cause teachers to fail; we cause their students to fail, too.

Let's insist that schools focus on academics

Understanding that the central role of schools—their priority—is helping all the children who can become competent in academics to reach reasonable goals will lead to more sensible public education policies. If it's taken seriously, this understanding will lead to a focus on proper instruction in academic skills and on the insistence that teachers use instructional methods that have the strongest basis in carefully designed field tests. We want our children to learn many things, but the priority of the schools is to teach academic skills to all who can learn them. The other things schools do is secondary to academic instruction.

But, remember, nonacademic self-care skills are also critically important for those who can't learn academic skills. Focusing on students' presence in the general education classroom at the expense of these critical skills is a tragicomic breach of public trust. For these students, school must be about learning the basics of taking care of oneself. And, inevitably, there will be kids who need instruction in some of both—some academics, some self-care. We want all kids to become all they can be, and the schools should help them learn all they can.

As I've suggested, schools must be seen first and foremost as being about academic learning for those who can become competent in academics. They can't avoid that responsibility and be found accountable to the larger society. The larger society can't establish sensible policies regarding schools that are based on some other premise—that schools are primarily responsible for something else. And there is a reasonable limit to what can be expected of schools, just as there is a reasonable limit to what *any* institution can do.

Predictably and understandably, some good, intelligent people will disagree with me about the role of schools in our society. Such disagreement isn't only to be expected but valued as part of the dissent that makes democratic institutions what they are. Ultimately, what schools are for and the policies that govern them are matters decided by the majority of those who participate in the political process. The political process works best when participants are well informed of the facts and doggedly analytical in dealing with problems. This assumption guides all of the chapters in this book.

Notes for Chapter Seven

[1] Mark Twain (2004) *Following the Equator*, chapter LXI, "Pudd'nhead Wilson's New Calendar"

[2] Neider (1917/1966, p. 13)

[3] Neider (1917/1966, p. 13)

[4] Mark Twain Foundation (1967, p. 63)

[5] Wagoner (2004, p. 14)

[6] Pulliam & Van Patten (2003)

[7] Twain & Warner (1874/2008, p. 41)

[8] Hirsch (1987)

[9] Hirsch (1996), Ravitch (2000)

[10] See Engelmann (1969), Engelmann, Bateman, & Lloyd (2007), Grossen (1993), Hirsch (1996), Kauffman (2002)

[11] See Kauffman (2005, 2008), Kauffman & Konold (2009), Rothstein, Jacobsen, & Wilder (2006)

[12] See Mungazi (1999), Watras (2004)

[13] Dorn (2007)

[14] Kauffman, Conroy, Gardner, & Oswald (2008)

[15] See Ryan & Cooper (2004), Part I; see also Kauffman (2002), Will (2001b, 2008)

[16] See Engelmann et al. (2007), Grossen (1993), Hirsch (1996), Kauffman (2002), Kauffman, Mock, Mostert, & Kavale (2008), and Mock & Kauffman (2002, 2005) for discussion of issues in teacher training and illogical ideas about teaching and learning

[17] Kauffman, Mock, Mostert, & Kavale (2008)

[18] Ravitch (2000)

[19] Mungazi (1999, p. 210)

[20] Rothman & Berkowitz (1967)

[21] See Engelmann (1969)

[22] Engelmann (1969, p. 30)

[23] Kauffman, Conroy, et al. (2008)

[24] Kundera (1990)

Part II
Thinking and Fixing

Chapter Eight:
Better Thinking about Standardized Tests

How Better Thinking About Tests Can Help Us Improve Our Understanding of Schools

Language and thought are closely linked. The first step toward doing something constructive about the tragicomedy that public education has become—after we've had a good laugh at the comic part—is to improve our own thinking. We must demand better thinking of ourselves and others; we must use clear, reality-based language in describing educational problems and their solutions. And *we have to improve our thinking about what standardized tests can and can't do—why we need them and how they can be used sensibly.*

In this chapter, we'll turn to thinking about standardized testing because it's become the focal point for much controversy. By "standardized" I mean that the same test is given to a large and supposedly representative sample of children . . . on which it is then standardized, or normed. Tests measure what students can do. Standardized tests of achievement are like standardized measurements of temperature, weight, or other scales that help us judge a child's health. And we need standards against which we can judge students' academic performance. *Standardized tests are the best and perhaps the only measures we have for making judgments about whether our students have met some of the goals we set, but we have to realize that not all students can meet a given standard.*

Granted, we need other kinds of measures of what students can do, but we simply can't know everything we need to know without standardized tests. Here's the simple truth: the idea of getting rid of standardized tests is just ridiculous; these tests are essential, but they need to be used wisely and understood better. We simply must know how kids are doing compared to others in our state, if not the nation, and we can't know that without standardized tests.

Good teachers check frequently to see what their students have learned. That is, they *measure* outcomes. Their testing is curriculum-referenced or curriculum-based, and the results tell teachers if students know or can do what they've been taught. This kind of testing is far more frequent and useful than federal- or state-mandated testing that occurs every year or so. In fact, you could say that assessment or measurement—a check to see whether the student grasps the idea or can perform as expected—is built into the lessons of effective teachers.

There is no substitute for this kind of nearly continuous testing.[1] It's a regular part of competent educational practice, special and general. But this kind of testing by teachers, like standardized testing, can't do the job alone. My major point stands: *what standardized testing can tell us is critical to improving our schools, and we ignore or misunderstand it at our peril.*

Misunderstandings about tests

Sometimes standardized test results are used erroneously to represent things they clearly don't. For example, a school's standardized test scores might be interpreted to mean that the school is a failure when it isn't. It might be judged a failure simply because one subgroup didn't meet an unreasonable expectation or because it fell below the median for the state while the statistical reality is that half the schools in a state will be below that state's median. Or a school's high test score averages might be interpreted to mean that all its students were well taught, while its students with disabilities, or its gifted students, or both, got very ineffective teaching. And too often, dodgy judgments like these are made on the basis of test scores alone. But criticizing standardized tests because they're misused doesn't justify eliminating them. The fact is, they're a cornerstone of educational integrity. Describing tests as monstrous, as some have done, or calling for their abandonment is counterproductive. Without them we'd have no systematic or objective way of knowing how students are doing compared to others. Then we'd never get public education back on track.

How people think they can work toward educational equity without tests to measure what kids have learned beats me. Though mismeasurement is indeed common, measurement is essential; while it's true that we can't misuse information we don't have, neither can we use it well. And test information is critical for our evaluation and implementation of educational best practices.

Standardized and infrequent teacher testing both have limitations. Yearly tests tell us too late what should have been taught. By the time we look at standardized test scores, the problem has already happened. Standardized tests tell teachers too late what they *should* have taught. But that's not the main thing that standardized tests are supposed to do. They're supposed to assess big-picture school and student performance. Infrequent teacher-made tests have the same disadvantage—telling teachers what they *should* have taught. This doesn't mean yearly or grading-period tests shouldn't be used. Yearly standardized tests tell us things that infrequently-given teacher-made and frequently-given curriculum-based tests can't. They show how the student compares to others. For bottom-line performance assessments, it'll always be important to know how a pupil or a class, school, district, or state is doing compared to the average.

But damning standardized tests simply makes no sense. People can do dumb things with data from test scores, but that doesn't invalidate testing. Not wanting to know how a child is doing, as compared to the norm, whether in education or in physiology, is a lapse of common sense that's close to criminal.

Test results are often hard to figure out, and sometimes we don't understand them, but that's often because they haven't been sufficiently explained. Test scores, like stock prices, aren't helpful if you don't know how to interpret them, and a lot of people in high places have low-level skills when it comes to making sense of test data. This gives testing an undeserved bad name. Regardless of the reason for your interest in schools, you need to recognize some realities about tests.

Realities applying to all tests

Let's consider a few of the things we know about measuring educational performance (testing). First of all, you get an average. Every single time. But you also get some other statistical-mathematical realities that we won't go into here. These statistical "moments," as statisticians call them, include central tendency, variability, skew, and kurtosis, and if you want to know more about any of them you can either go to a basic statistics text or go online and find out about them.[2]

For our purposes here, we just need to consider averages and percentile ranks on any test. One kind of average comes from adding up scores and dividing by the number of people taking the test. This is called the mean (or arithmetic mean). It's affected by extremes. Here's an example to illustrate how extremes can affect a mean. Suppose that in a neighborhood, five people have the following annual incomes: $25,000, $30,000, $35,000, $40,000, $50,000, and $250,000. If you add these up and divide by 5, you get $86,000. Now, $86,000 is the arithmetic mean, and it's an average, but is it representative of the incomes of the five families in that neighborhood? No! That person with the $250,000 income skewed the average and made it higher than anyone else's. Another kind of average is the middle score—the median, the 50th percentile. In the neighborhood I just mentioned, $40,000 is the median annual income, and the median is way more representative of the incomes of the people who live there. Partly, that's because someone actually had that income! The 50th percentile—the middle score—is often preferred to the mean because it's less affected by extreme scores. Think about this in terms of a classroom. If the IQ scores of five kids are 85, 90, 95, 100, and 160, what's more representative of the class? The arithmetic average (106) or the median (95)?

A distribution always—no exceptions—has percentiles. A percentile just means that a certain percentage of the individuals taking the test were at or below a certain value—any kid taking a test might be at or below a given test score. *Percentile* means taking hundredths (or a percent) of the distribution. It divides the distribution into hundredths, giving you a scale of 1 to 100 for comparison. So, for example, on a test the 88th percentile means that 88 percent of test takers got that score or a lower one; 12 percent got a higher score.

Percentiles and other statistics tell us important things about how a school or class or student compares to the norm. But comparisons can also be cockeyed. Here are two ways in which standardized test scores can be helpful:

1. Schools and school systems can compare their average scores to state or national norms to get a better idea of subjects in the curriculum in which they're doing better or worse than average.

2. Classroom teachers can judge the progress of individual students to see how they compare to others.

But, remember, we can make comparisons and then do very unintelligent things based on them. Here are two ways in which standardized test scores can be misused or abused:

1. Schools can be called failures or underperforming based on test scores alone when they're actually doing okay.

2. Teachers or students can be criticized for having done a miserable job on the basis of the test scores alone when they've done just fine.

We have to be careful how we use test scores so we don't reach indefensible conclusions. Much of the misunderstanding and misuse of test scores is based on a misunderstanding of what norms represent—how they're obtained, what they mean, and how we judge progress or lack of it. A norm defines the way something like height or weight or temperature or academic achievement is distributed.

We judge people to be tall or obese or feverish or low achievers according to a standard—according to measures that give us averages and extremes. As I'll mention later, a judgment of "tall" is made only in relation to a measure of height that tells us what's average and what's not. And what was once considered "tall" is today average or short because the norm has changed. Likewise, what's considered "average" achievement today might not be considered "average" in 25 years; "average" achievement is "average" only when compared to a particular group. Garrison Keillor's description of Lake Wobegon is funny because we understand that only in some fantasy world are all of the children above average. We think, "Average compared to whom?" and we understand that you can't have everyone above average in any reasonable comparison. If "average" is defined by the kids in Lake Wobegon, then we understand that every kid in Lake Wobegon being above that average is pure goofiness. But even if we assume "average" is defined by kids everywhere, Lake Wobegon is unlike any real place of any size when no kids who live there are below the national average.

So sure, we can use norms to help us figure out how well schools or systems or teachers or kids are doing. Only we have to be aware of what we're comparing them to and the realities of norms. It's common for us to hear people say that our students should score higher compared to others—their percentile ranks on a standardized test should go up. Okay so far. But, you also have to consider that when you "norm" a test by giving it to a large, representative group of students, 30 percent of the students taking *that* test at *that* time scored at the 30th percentile or lower. The 30th percentile means that 30 percent got that score or lower in the norming process. You can't have more than 70 percent above the 30th percentile *in that normative group*. True, a student or a group may get better scores *compared to their previous performance on standardized tests*. And improving those scores is good. But you also have to realize that when you start comparing schools, teachers, or students to each other, they can't all be at the top. That defies the very definition of a norm. Even more important is the fact that they can't *all* be above average or *all* be better than those at any other point above the bottom.

This becomes a problem—and a serious one—in setting state or national standards (assuming the norm is for the state or nation) and expecting *all* of the students (or schools) to score above a certain percentile greater than 1. That just can't happen because of realities— those of basic mathematics and the way the world works. Some students will score very low because of their disability, or because they were not well taught, or because they refused to take the test or botched it, or for reasons we don't understand. In any group tested in any way, someone will bring up the rear. That's just a reality. On any test, some students will be low scorers compared to others. That, too, is a reality. So the goal of "universal proficiency" really is the pursuit of a phantom, a will-o'-the-wisp that legislators and educators or anyone else who thinks about this should understand.[3] And the fact that some students or teachers compare unfavorably to others on any given criterion doesn't mean they're failures, as I'll discuss later.

This becomes a serious problem when people call for higher standards *and* lower rates of failure. A standard—a set criterion, usually expressed as a percentile on a standardized test or other measure—means that those who haven't reached it have failed in some way. They haven't "measured up." Setting any comparative standard inevitably creates failures, simply because of comparisons based on the measurement. Setting a higher standard creates more failures to "measure up." Unless the measurement that you get when you test a given group is phony—outdated or inaccurate—that's the way measurement works. Want a higher standard? Then brace yourself: in *this* world, that means you're courting yet more failure.

The lives of norms

Statistical distributions or "norms" often change over time, but sometimes they don't. "Normal" body temperature hasn't changed much in the past century, but the "normal" height of adults has changed a lot. Normative age at death—what we call "life expectancy"—now is a lot longer than it used to be. Sometimes norms change; sometimes the change is good, and sometimes it's bad.

To take an obvious example of a norm that *has* changed for the better over time, the average height of American people over the past 200 years has increased significantly, probably owed in large measure to better nutrition. Another normative change is the increased average life span of Americans. So should a man who's 5 feet 10 inches tall consider himself tall or a woman 75 years of age consider herself to have lived to a ripe old age? All depends on whether you want to make a comparison to old norms or recent ones. And what should we consider "normal" weight? Just because the average weight: height ratio has gone up doesn't mean that a child who was considered obese 25 years ago shouldn't be now. Obesity could be judged by comparison to a normative distribution of weight:height ratios, but that doesn't mean that the current norm is the best one. Probably, we'd be better off not

considering today's average weight:height ratios to be the standard for judging obesity.

The same kind of choice applies when we think about norms having to do with educational tests. Do norms go out of date? Of course they sometimes do! That's why, from time to time, we need new norms on things like the SAT or any other test. A norm depends on who takes the test. If only a select group of high achievers takes a test, then the mean of the normative group will be relatively high—higher than when just about everybody takes the test, meaning that the low achievers take it, too. Some people forget that the norm for high school students on academic tests was for a *far* more selective group in 1909 than in 2009 because a comparatively small percentage of the population went to high school in 1909.

In some ways, a statistical distribution or norm is like a snapshot, a picture of reality for a particular group at a particular time. It's important to consider just who's in the "snapshot" or norm group. For educational testing, this means we have to consider things like gender, ethnic group, prior education, socioeconomic status, and so on. We're not making good sense if we compare an individual or a group to a norm that didn't include people like them. You get the absurdity of comparing a young child's height and weight to a norm for adults. It's just as silly to compare the test scores of kids who've had little opportunity to learn something to a norm for kids who've had lots of opportunities to learn it.

So we have to make sure our comparisons are to norms that are right for (1) the time, and (2) the individual or group. Of course, there's always the complaint that a comparison is unfair because the normative group didn't include kids (or enough of them) in a particular category. Sometimes this complaint is fully justified; sometimes it isn't. True, tests can be "biased" toward or against certain groups in their norms. The fact that they *can* be doesn't mean that they *are*.

Comparing individuals and groups

Remember, a norm is like a snapshot. Individuals might be standing or sitting in a different *place* in the group. The same goes for groups or clusters of individuals. Their place can shift. Even their relative height or weight can change. But here's another reality: people can't get younger or older than others in the group. So their relative ages can't change at all. Yes, people die or don't show up for the picture, so they're not included. But a statistical snapshot isn't exactly like that—

unless we're willing to exclude people. And even if we do, we've got to deal with the realities of the group we've caught "on camera."

In a statistical snapshot known as a norm, people can change their location in the group (i.e., their percentile rank), but the norm, the whole distribution, is something we have to deal with. The norm still has its statistical "moments" or mathematical realities that just won't go away. It still has a median; percentiles still apply. You still can't have more than 50 percent above the median; you still can't avoid having a 10th percentile or any other percentile from 1 to 100.

Regardless of how long we've used it or who it includes, a norm (or normative distribution) is a statistical template to which we compare an individual or group. We might find that an individual or group has changed compared to the norm. A student who used to be in the bottom third of the norm might now be in the top third, for example. A student might gain or lose compared to the norm you're using. The same could happen with a group. So we might say, "Wow, that kid really made a big improvement!" or "Well, that group didn't make any improvement at all!" compared to a norm.

Here's the kicker for making comparisons and judging progress: in rankings or comparisons there are certain realities you just can't change. For example, you can't compare schools to each other on a given scale and then find that there aren't top schools and bottom schools, schools that rank high and low, or, if you want NCLB-speak, successful schools and failing schools.

Why we need statistics

Statistics are as real and as useful as our most vital innovations, including houses, computers, roads, laws, and languages. They can be used well, but they can also be abused. And we should understand that some of the things we know about them can change but others can't. We need statistics to help us figure out the meanings of comparisons among individuals and groups, but we have to understand that comparisons become nonsensical when we ignore what a statistic means.

When we make comparisons among them, we know that half the states (in the nation), half the school districts (in the state), and half the schools (in the district) are going to be below the median (the middle score) and many will be below the mean (the arithmetic average) for the nation, state, and district respectively on whatever we measure.

Furthermore, it means that there will always be test score gaps of some description and size between various nations, states, school districts, schools, and groups of students. And this in turn implies that revealed and unfair realities should be rectified. Some gaps are a result of children's neglect and abuse, some gaps are attributable to poor teaching, and some gaps can and should be narrowed or closed, especially gaps that are a result of inadequate education. We have to realize that in some "under-resourced" schools the kids don't even have the books they need!

But it really doesn't matter what anyone (president, secretary of education, Congress, advisor, school superintendent, education "expert") says or wants or has written into policy, measurements are going to correspond to those statistical "moments" in the real world of test scores. Understanding this is part of our reality check on judgments of progress. Yes, we should close the gaps we can, but thinking that all gaps are the same or that all gaps are closable is a fool's proposition.

Where benchmarks come from

The academic criteria used to categorize students are often based on measurement of their performance on standardized tests. This is often reasonable. However, a policy assuming that all students will become proficient, which means be able to perform at a specified level greater than a certain score greater than zero (say, the score that is at the 25th percentile), is dead on arrival. There are two reasons for this: (1) unless a criterion greater than zero doesn't represent reality, you can't have all the test-takers above it, and (2) what we know about reality is that some kids, who nonetheless deserve our respect and concern, are going to score zero or very low on the test—certainly below that criterion score that is chosen to represent "proficient."

It's important to understand that criteria for graduation (or promotion or a certain diploma or anything else) or what we often call "benchmarks" aren't just pulled out of the air. Benchmarks or judgments of high performance aren't considered high or good without reference to a statistical distribution of test scores. I repeat: criteria or benchmarks are ultimately related to normative distributions. We may be able to avoid considering normative distributions for a while, but not for long in the real world. In the real world, a higher benchmark means that, in the distribution of those tested, fewer will reach it. You want more than 75 percent of kids to score higher than the 25th percentile? Well, then do one of two things: (1) compare the kids to an

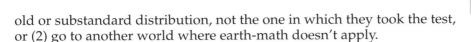

old or substandard distribution, not the one in which they took the test, or (2) go to another world where earth-math doesn't apply.

Think about this, too: people can play sly games with benchmarks. They can claim that students in a particular group or school or district or state have improved because a larger percentage met a benchmark (like "proficient" or "graduated"). But they might have moved the mark—moved it lower or made it easier—or simply ignored the outliers (those at the bottom of the heap). It's really hard to show improvement and not cheat if you think you can get away with it. Like students, all of us will do what we can to make ourselves and our policies look good.

Remember Mark Twain's observation that he'd seen a lot of legislatures and in each he observed that a comfortable majority knew just about enough to come in out of the rain, and that was all?[4] Well, we need to think better than the legislators and blowhards who imagine that we can actually achieve universal proficiency. I think it's fair to assume that when it comes to policies like NCLB, legislators who think it's a good idea "got some 'splainin' to do." Maybe it just slipped their minds that statistics actually apply to tests and that some kids actually have disabilities that mean they're not going to become "proficient" in reading or math—ever. If so, we need to remind them.

More inconvenient truths about tests and testing

Some people apparently would like to test educational performance precisely and find no variance—no detectable differences in measurements, no failures, and no gaps between groups or schools. But as far as I can figure out, there are only two ways to do that: (1) measure (or test) very imprecisely, so that everything or everyone measured falls into the same category, or (2) don't actually test at all.

Any reasonably precise measurement (or test) puts some people or things above and some below average on whatever is measured. You can't produce a distribution in which all the test takers are above the average; it's just a mathematical impossibility, the way the world is. As mentioned, that's why we laugh at Keillor's Lake Wobegon, where all the children are above average. And if the distribution is skewed by the high performers, then it's a mathematical certainty that more than half of the test takers will be below the arithmetic average (mean) for that distribution. It's just basic math—the fundamental statistical stuff that can't be changed just because somebody doesn't like it.

Not liking the way statistics work could be compared to not liking the gap between two integers, say 5 and 6. We know that fractions exist, but let's suppose you deny their existence or relevance. If you did that, you could also deny there is a gap between 5 and 6. But your denial of a gap between 5 and 6 doesn't close it or make it go away. Yet much education policy is comparable to not liking the gap between 5 and 6 but wanting to admit the reality of fractions anyway. You simply can't have it both ways. You want all gaps closed? Then give up the idea of numbers as we know them!

To some, ignorance is, indeed, bliss. That is, they're happier not knowing how a child compares to others (or the average) and not knowing what the distribution of test scores is. And the fact is that it's hard for any of us to confront the reality that our child is low compared to the average in anything—that we or someone we love compares unfavorably to most others in the population. We'd rather focus on the things in which we or our loved ones compare favorably. That's natural, but it can lead to a rejection of reality if we're not careful. Some of us—and we deserve ridicule for this if we're intelligent adults—are very good at ignoring reality or truth about standardized tests and urging others to do so as well.[5]

Assessing educational progress

When you're trying to assess the progress of a student in a curriculum, the most important comparison is the student's own performance over time. You need to know whether the student is improving and if the student's performance shows a trend toward increasing competence or fluency in the skill you're teaching. And not just that. You also need to know whether a trend line showing improvement is steep enough for the student to catch up to the average. The objective of special education is to accelerate learning so kids can catch up to their same-age peers when possible.[6]

Nevertheless, and sad but true, some students are nonresponders to the best instruction we can offer. Good teachers keep trying, but sometimes the student just doesn't learn as much as we'd like, and we don't always know why. This is true in both general and special education. Thus, it's a certainty that some students will remain below average by any reasonable comparison, and some will fail to make significant progress even when their own prior test performance is the only criterion.

When trying to see if a student is meeting a reasonable expectation, comparison to others' test scores is essential. Otherwise, we have no way of knowing if an expectation is reasonable. This is so commonsensical, it's embarrassing to have to point it out, but some educators seem to favor an alternative assumption. Without norms for growth, temperature, math, reading, and so on, we simply don't know when someone is doing what most do, or is way high or too low.

This isn't solely a mathematical process, and I'm not saying that reasonable expectations shouldn't take the individual into account. The peculiarities of personality always are variable. Expecting a student to achieve like most kids his or her age could be way, way off—totally unreasonable. Our expectation could be ridiculously high or low, depending on the child.

Making the right comparisons is important, but so is interpreting the results. How much difference in test scores is significant or important? How much difference should trigger action? No measurement is perfect, so how much is random and predictable error on any test? Which test score differences should result in our asking, "Who cares?" because they're so small, and which are legitimate reasons for elation or serious concern because they're so big? We really don't know without knowing the size of the statistically predictable error on the test. Too often, news media, politicians, and educators make something of nothing or miss an important difference when reporting test score releases. Too often—perhaps because of a slow news day—a big deal is made about a change in ranking or a few points on a test, results that weren't statistically or practically significant in the first place. On the other hand, a result of whopping significance may simply be ignored by the press . . . perhaps on a busy news day or with a less-than-observant education editor.

The issue of significant change in test scores is critically important for programs designed to either reward schools that improve or close down schools that fail. Further, we always need to ask what index of central tendency (average) serves as the basis for "improvement" or "failure"—for example, the mean (arithmetic average) or the median (the middle score)? And how much change could be just random error—what statisticians call a standard error of measurement?

Another important thing to ask about is what happened to those at the margins of the distribution—those whose scores are particularly high or low? Could a school be judged to have "improved" by raising its average while neglecting students with exceptionally low scores? It would, of course, be possible to "succeed" by raising the average while producing no improvement at all in the scores of the low performers. The same would apply to high performers because in either case, those in the middle have more potential to improve the average because of their sheer numbers. So if your goal is simply to survive, it's tempting to forget those at the extremes. In fact, this appears to be exactly what some so-called "successful" schools do.[7] In other words, deciding whether or not a school is successful depending on the cut scores that define "proficiency" is inadequate and misleading.[8]

What comparisons should we make?

So, to what populations (or distributions) should we compare ourselves or our schools or students? It depends on what we want to know and what we want to make of the comparison. If I compared my bass playing to that of professional players, I'd look really bad and want to give up. Probably I'd engage in a lot of self-derogatory thinking. Or, I could compare my bass playing to that of others who, like me, started playing relatively late in life (age 55). In that case, I might feel pretty good. Or, if I wanted to make myself look really good, I'd compare my bass playing to that of people my age who've never touched a bass in their lives. Then there's the matter of which proficiency is being tested. Depends on whether it's simply plucking an open string or playing a difficult symphony.

The point is, in education we often find silly comparisons—apples to oranges, or worse. It may make sense to judge progress by comparison to national norms of achievement on standardized tests, but let's not avoid this reality: once we get a lot of students above the national norm, the norm will be judged "outdated" and a new norm will take its place. Sometimes I wonder why education critics don't just compare current student performances to way old norms, declare schools "fixed," and stop complaining. I've also wondered how these critics would know that the schools have been "fixed" in the first place, because their concept of "fix" doesn't correspond to statistical realities. Some critics have even compared present-day expectations to earlier expectations on tasks that schools no longer consider important. Remember, to make sense you'd have to compare those who were tested in the old days to a similar group of students today; lots of students didn't go to school or weren't included in old norms. There are many ways to make silly or unhelpful comparisons, and they're too often made for all the wrong reasons.

Obsession with being first, best, highest, #1 on any test in any way you choose to say it may be peculiarly American. Whether it is or not, it's clear that American politicians want American education at all levels, as reflected by test scores, to be judged the best in the world (American higher education is often thus judged; it's K–12 education that's depicted in many comparisons as far less than best). But here's a hard reality: test comparisons of any kind always put someone (or something) lowest or last and someone (or something) highest or at the top. And half will be below the median—unless the comparison is made to another group's distribution.

Regardless of obsessing about being #1, the fact remains that test score comparisons will always put someone last, meaning that any program designed to eliminate "failure," as defined by being last or lowest, is doomed itself to fail. By definition, someone will always finish last and therefore failure by comparison to a norm won't be eliminated. Seems obvious, but that doesn't keep the U. S. Congress, states, secretaries of education, politicians, and school board members from proposing it or the public from buying into the opposite!

Is it okay for someone to be lowest? I think it all depends. Being last or lowest should be no cause for alarm in education if those individuals are still doing their best, and particularly if their performance is good for them, though not as good as others'. We often make too much out of being first or last or above or below average. What it *means* to be first or last or average depends on the distribution you're comparing to. Consider, too, that not everyone can be first or above average, and being lowest isn't always to have failed in a meaningful way. It depends on your objectives. Still, most of us, most of the time and for good reason, want to know how we compare to others.

The reality and difficulty of borders

Anytime we define an acceptable level of performance, some individuals are on the edge of it. That is, they're "borderline," and judgments about which side of the line they're on will sometimes be wrong. Although this might be self-evident, some people make too much of it. Those who object to this observation or to any measurement or test that produces it (and every measurement produces this effect) want things to be clear-cut: on or off, black or white, 0 or 1, as in a computer chip's memory. But most human characteristics are continuously distributed—that is, they have values that range from a little to a lot with really fine gradations of the variable being possible. Height, for example, is continuously distributed, as is weight, age,

skin color, reading ability, and intelligence. You can have itsy-bitsy differences as well as big ones. Some things, like citizenship, have discrete variables. They're one way or the other, and you can't find something that's only "just a little bit." That's why we laugh about being "a little bit pregnant"—you either are or you aren't; you can't be a little bit. Consider citizenship. You are legally a citizen or not. There's no in-between. But, again, most things we test in education are continuous variables, not categorical (discrete) variables.

For any continuously distributed variable, we set a cut-off value that seems reasonable, although people who come close to it don't quite make it or qualify. "Tall" is an arbitrary distinction that has value, but if we say a tall person is 6 feet 4 inches in height, then by definition someone who is 6 feet 3 inches is what? Average height? Short? We make countless judgments by comparison to arbitrary standards. Sometimes we put people in discrete categories based on a continuously distributed variable that can be precisely measured. That still leaves some people on the cusp, the almost-but-not-quite—tall/short, fat/thin, rich/poor, and so on. And to the extent that we consider many variables at once and form a judgment based on the general picture—competent or not competent for a particular job, for instance—we are especially likely to find different people arriving at different conclusions about the same case. For example, one interviewer might judge a given interviewee "competent," yet another "not competent."

Disabilities are just arbitrary designations, somebody's judgment about where to draw the line for low vision or hearing or physical limitation or intellectual ability and so on. So why do some people have such a hard time with so-called "judgmental" disabilities, as if some are *not* judgmental? By judgmental disabilities, people apparently mean those in which test scores are most obviously open to criticism, such as learning disabilities, emotional or behavioral disorders, giftedness, or mental retardation. Beats me why they have a problem with these categories, at least in most cases. Could be they just don't like the judgments people make. They disagree about particular cases. Fine, but then it's the specific judgment, not the fact that judgment or testing is required, that they should complain about.

Measurement can be faulty, testing inadequate, judgment way off, and so on. But this isn't the same as criticizing a category of performance or ability simply because people may disagree on who belongs in it and who doesn't. Or that some kids are on the border of a cut point in test scores. There isn't any way to take all of the ambiguity out of teaching or out of categorizing students. And there isn't any way to avoid categories, which are often referred to as "pigeon-holes" by those who complain about them.

What kind of mistake is worse?

It's important to consider the costs of making certain kinds of mistakes. Suppose we're considering whether to identify a student for a special program based on test scores. If we identify a student we shouldn't, then our mistake is a false positive. If we don't identify a student whom we should, then our mistake is a false negative. Which is worse? All depends on how you view being identified—the advantages and the personal costs and risks involved if you make one mistake versus the other. Of course, there are the clear-cut cases, but that's not the point here. The point is that in some cases we won't know for sure what to do. There's no way around this. It goes with the realities of measuring or testing. It's a part of education, special or general, that can't be avoided.

Let's think better about tests and testing

Better thinking about tests and testing will help us improve our schools and improve both general and special education if we understand why tests are given, the advantages and limitations of different kinds of tests, and what's mathematically possible when we test various groups of students. Someone has evidence that a given test is bad? Then let them present that evidence and suggest or make a better test. If they can't do either, they should quit carping about testing.

Nothing is to be gained—in fact, much is to be lost—when policy makers, parents, or educators themselves talk or write as if testing itself is the problem. NCLB is not a problem because it calls for testing but because it expects test scores that are out of sync with reality. Unless we're willing to shoot the brightest kids and the slowest learners too—or at least not test them—and offer really miserable instruction to the rest, no state can possibly produce the no-gap test scores NCLB says we should aim for.

Really, if you want to know how kids are doing, then you have to measure (test) their performance. If you want to know how they're doing compared to others, then all the kids to be compared have to take the same test. And if you give a group of kids the same test, there's going to be a distribution of test scores with immutable mathematical properties. Every single time, no exceptions. It's basic math. Sorry. That's just the way it is.

Notes for Chapter Eight

[1] See Deno (1997) and Fuchs & Fuchs (2001)

[2] Kauffman & Konold (2007), Konold & Kauffman (2009); see also any basic textbook on statistics

[3] Rothstein, Jacobson, & Wilder (2006)

[4] Day (1966, p. 109); for further discussion of the use of statistics in educational decisions, request of the author the article by Kauffman and Lloyd (2009)

[5] For example, Kohn (2000, 2001)

[6] Kauffman & Hallahan (2005a)

[7] Cook, Gerber, & Semmel (1997)

[8] See Ho (2008) for discussion of why statistical analyses should involve the whole distribution, not just cut scores

Part II
Thinking and Fixing

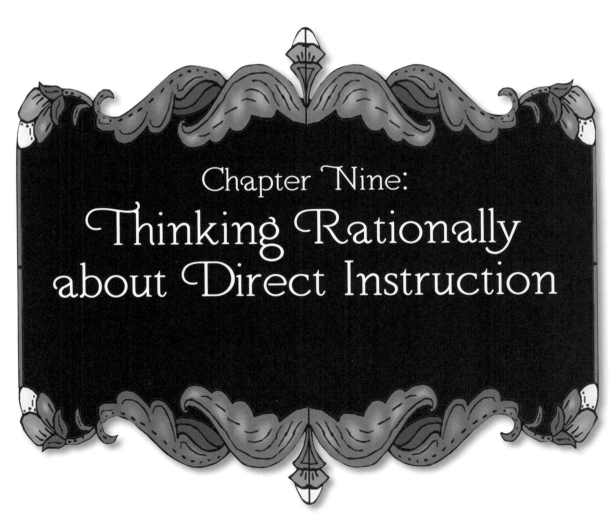

Chapter Nine:
Thinking Rationally about Direct Instruction

How Rational Thinking about Direct Instruction Can Make Schools More Effective

While nothing in education works all the time, there's no doubt that some things work far better than others. Yet people are fooled into thinking that because something—no matter how crack-brained it may be—*appears* to have worked at least once, that's sufficient proof of its effectiveness. This may come from firsthand experience, or from received wisdom—hearsay. And it too often results in heartwarming, but nonetheless apocryphal, testimony. This highly personal yet wholly unscientific testimony then can be used to prey on the hopes and fears of others. Especially parents, because they so yearn for support for their struggling children that they're easily misled into believing in instructional dead ends. And if personal testimony isn't doing the trick, parents may be tricked by ersatz "research" that's never been subjected to the harsh scrutiny of science.

Yet *direct instruction is known to work and is supported by reliable, empirical evidence.* Unbelievably, it comes as a surprise to some that we can actually make discriminations among instructional programs selected on evidence-based outcomes where evidence (data) strongly suggests that some approaches are significantly better than others for achieving particular goals.[1]

Thinking about what works and what doesn't

Here are misstatements of fact that some people inexplicably seem to hold dear, including many who should know better:

1. Nothing works in education.

2. Nor are there particular programmatic approaches that work better than others.

3. Because nothing works better than anything else and one approach is as good as another, we may as well toss teachers a "grab-bag" of ideas, expose them to all available methodologies, and let them figure out what works.

What a muddle-headed way of looking at the world, especially when it comes to education! Here's, in fact, what we are reasonably certain about:

1. Some instructional approaches work far better than others and have been scientifically proven to be more effective.

2. We must teach teachers what works and what doesn't.

3. We often waste teacher/student time and effort on approaches proven not to work.

The fact that nothing works every time and everything appears to work sometimes shouldn't stop us from choosing what's *most likely to work most of the time*. And we need always to have plans B, C, etc., when plan A doesn't succeed. Then, on those relatively rare occasions when we aren't successful with our first choice, we're prepared to move efficiently to the next one. But we don't abandon reason or start trying things at random, responses generally associated with incompetence and panic. We expect physicians, pilots, mechanics, and other professionals to try the best-tested, most-likely-to-work things first and to move systematically from there through the hierarchy of backup plans. Teachers should approach problems no differently.

Okay, if not random selection, then what should we select? Simple: the best selection is the instructional strategy with the strongest support in scientifically based field trials. What's the best bet for getting the results we want from the greatest percentage of students? And what's the best bet we have today? These are the questions we ought to be asking, not what's the most popular or the most "intuitive" to someone, the most consistent with our political views, or the most consistent with an educational philosophy. If we don't ask these questions and answer them objectively, then we end up wasting a lot of money—and wasting teacher/student time—on things only a fool would support. Equally as bad, our failure to select the best that today's scientific evidence supports invites postmodern nonsense and ineffective methods to fill the void.

The folly of mixing up politics and good teaching

Now, if you want the views of a humorist who, like Mark Twain, often uses his wit for serious purpose, you might turn to an essay by Garrison Keillor (for January 30, 2008; see first website listed for Chapter 9). It includes some pithy comments on reading instruction. He suggests that it's difficult for a liberal Democrat to share ideas about education with Republicans. But, he says:

> Reading is the key to everything. Teaching children to read is a fundamental moral obligation of the society. That 27 percent are at serious risk of crippling illiteracy is an outrageous scandal.

> . . . Nice people are failing these kids, but when they are called on it, they get very huffy. When the grand poobah PhDs of education stand up and blow, they speak with great confidence about theories of teaching, and considering the test results, the bums ought to be thrown out.

> There is much evidence that teaching phonics really works, especially with kids with learning disabilities, a growing constituency. But because phonics is associated with behaviorism and with conservatives, and because the Current Occupant [George W. Bush, at that time] has spoken on the subject, my fellow liberals are opposed.

> Liberal dogma says that each child is inherently gifted and will read if only he is read to . . . Democrats . . . should take another look at the Reading First program. It is morally disgusting if Democrats throw out Republican programs that are good for children. Life is not a scrimmage. Grown-ups who stick with dogma even though it condemns children to second-class lives should be put on buses and sent to North Dakota to hoe wheat for a year.

I agree. We should put away childish things. And perhaps nothing is more childish than opposing something just because it's associated with a political or philosophical view that we don't like. What's known as direct instruction (di) is a good bet. The approach known as Direct Instruction (DI) is an even better bet. If you do a web search, you're very likely to turn up the same things for direct instruction and Direct Instruction. The difference signified by small vs. capital letters may be minor in some respects, but it's significant and requires some explanation.

Differences between di and DI

Direct instruction (sometimes called small d, small i, or systematic instruction) is based on the notion that you should teach skills and concepts directly, not just let kids explore things and "construct their own knowledge," as suggested by some educational philosophies, often called "holistic" or "constructivist." The principles of di are based on what we know from the best research we have about how children learn—research of cognitive processes.[2] It's not a matter of philosophy or politics but of the most objective evidence we can obtain.

The di approach includes things we know about the importance of review, presentation of new material, practice, and feedback. It stresses regular reviews of prior work before starting new lessons and periodic reviews to check overall retention. New material is presented with an explanation of where instruction is headed (goals), in small, logical steps that are modeled (demonstrated) and accompanied by clear language. In other words, students are never in doubt about where they're going in a lesson, and the idea is to teach directly (one-on-one when necessary) in ways students understand. The teacher using di gives positive (true) and negative (false) examples and checks to make sure every student understands each point. The teacher doesn't digress but stays on topic. A fast pace of instruction (but not so fast that students get lost) is also important in di. The di approach also includes practice guided by the teacher, lots of questions to which all students respond and receive feedback, a high rate of success (students "not getting it" usually means something is wrong with the teaching), and enough practice that students become fluent in the skill being taught. All di students get feedback about errors and correct responses. They are helped to give the correct response if they aren't sure. If the students aren't "getting it," then whatever they're not getting is retaught before moving on. The idea is to teach so that children learn, not merely "cover" material (from above, at 35,000 feet) or "find out for themselves" (why even go to school?). And students are given time for independent practice, too. The idea of this practice is to help them acquire the skill or idea being taught until it becomes automatic.

The program known as DI (or capital D, capital I) puts all of this into an explicit package.[3] It's a more structured version of di that's been field-tested. DI has taken the basic principles of di and applied them in explicit lessons to various aspects of curriculum at different levels. It includes programs to teach reading, math, and science. And because its lessons are written out ("scripted" or manualized), it's more consistent from teacher to teacher. DI has simply eaten the lunch of other

instructional approaches in field tests and therefore is a best-practices example of the superiority of a scientifically based instructional program. And yet, as I explain later, it hasn't been declared by the federal government to be any better than the competition, much of which is unmitigated hogwash!

Now, the idea of direct instruction (whether di or DI) may seem sensible to many people, but it's also been attacked as deadening, uncreative, restrictive, and philosophically wrong. A shameful part of the reason this is so, as Keillor suggests, is academic blow-hard bums with advanced degrees in education who object to both of these proven-superior approaches on ideological or philosophical grounds. They are the reason for this outrageous scandal that our policy makers have tolerated, as I suggest in the last chapter. Their tragicomic attacks are enough to make you crazy if you really care about kids learning all they can.

Teaching students letter-sound correspondence (basically, "phonics") through di or DI is a lot better bet, provably better, than "whole language" (now often dubbed "balanced instruction" or "balanced literacy" to cover its tracks because some people now know that "whole language" has failed miserably). While di and DI include reading for fun, the fun now comes on the back end because kids learn how to read more quickly and have more fun because their reading skills have improved significantly and they can now read material that was hitherto inaccessible to them. When they're taught reading skills *directly* instead of having the teacher read to them or turn them loose to learn by themselves, their fun is a result of having an advanced skill set. And wise teachers teach spelling *directly* so others know what students mean when they write. Teachers who're in the know don't approve of "invented spelling," an oxymoron if ever there was one. "Invented spelling" just makes them look incompetent. Students must be taught *directly* the difference between homonyms like peace/piece and son/sun. Teaching math facts and how to solve arithmetic problems *directly* gives them more skills more quickly than indirect, exploratory methods. And these skills provide the foundation for future learning.

But here we come to the real tragedy, unleavened by comedy: when people talk about school reform, they rarely even mention proper instruction, as if it barely matters. They focus on other things. Like bad teachers, these reformers get caught up in digressions. Like poor students, they're too easily distracted by peripheral issues and don't focus on the central idea.

The foolish focus of "reform"

For some reason, education reformers are hung up on form and forget about function—how and why *instruction* works. Here are the big topics: school choice, charters, vouchers, restructuring, annual testing, and standards of learning and inclusion, to name a few. All are doomed to fail at what reformers say they hope to achieve—better outcomes for all students—unless *instruction* gets better. And instruction doesn't automatically get better without specific attention to it. Perhaps a few students will improve when faced with demanding tests. A few parents will choose schools in which instruction is central. Some exceptional children will do very well in inclusion programs. But these will almost always be the students and parents who are already doing what we want. Most won't improve just because we expect them to. They won't make better choices just because choices are presented. They won't do these things, primarily, because they can't.

Consider, for example, the publication *Rethinking Special Education for a New Century*, an unwieldy, towering tome edited by Chester E. Finn, Jr., Andrew J. Rotherham, and Charles R. Hokanson, Jr., and published by the Fordham Foundation in 2001. Only one of its fifteen chapters bothers itself about what it regards as the relatively insignificant subject of instruction. The rest is about rules, compliance, state vs. national responsibilities, accountability (without saying, of course, that it's unconscionable to set standards without considering instruction and basic statistics), choice, administrative structures, eligibility for services, and assigning children to categories. In their final chapter on conclusions and principles for reform, Finn and his coworkers recommend six principles for reforming special education, which might be summarized as follows:

1. Make standards performance-based when possible.

2. Reduce the number of special education categories.

3. Focus on prevention and intervention, using research-based practices.

4. Encourage flexibility, innovation, and choice, giving parents and children options and fostering integration of general and special education.

5. Provide adequate funding.

6. End double standards whenever possible.

Here, where we supposedly get the big picture about educational reform—the most important stuff distilled—instruction is but a hint of a whisper. It's not made the central issue, but is reduced to a parenthetical comment: "Chapter 12 presents a compelling case for early identification, prevention, and intervention in what will otherwise emerge as learning disabilities. (This should, of course, be rooted in effective and research-based reading instruction.)"[4]

Or, consider an editorial published in the *Washington Post* on May 30, 2009, by William Brock, Ray Marshall, and Marc Tucker.[5] The authors list ten "steps" that they suggest will lead us to world-class schools, but not a single one deals with instruction. They do not consider the statistical realities involved in achieving their objectives, nor do they suggest how their suggestions would be paid for. Indeed, they propose "steps" to nowhere in the real world because they are simply not achievable regardless of the trillions of dollars that might be spent trying. Their suggestions are a cartoon-like fantasy, a caricature of serious discussion. This is not the kind of "thinking" we want our students to imitate.

The *focus* needs to be on instruction, not form or structure or testing, for reasons which seem obvious to me. Instruction fuels learning. Failing to pay attention to it is like failing to pay attention to what you're putting into your car's fuel tank. Instruction is the active ingredient in learning; it's the fuel, and yet those who focus on school restructuring—school choice, standards, inclusion, administrative forms of education— relegate it to secondary status. Or they ignore it completely. Yet among its many benefits, good instruction even lessens the probability that students will misbehave.[6]

The reason instruction receives so little attention in special education reform isn't hard to figure out. For one thing, reformers would have to boldly come out for the use of specific methods of instruction in general education, where most exceptional children spend a significant part of their time. That would require taking a stand. They would actually have to support particular methods of instruction that well-managed field tests show are most effective. They would also have to come out strongly and unambiguously for phonics-based direct instruction. This would require working against the popular affection for "progressive" education that E. D. Hirsch, Jr., and Diane Ravitch have so lovingly described.[7] And of course teachers would have to be trained or retrained, and that would cost money, displeasing those who want lower taxes. So yet another unpopular stand would have to be taken. Worse, some teachers and teacher educators want desperately to use or promote instructional methods that for strictly ideological reasons they favor. Because these methods aren't likely to have been proven effective, this would seriously put some noses out of joint.

What works and how to find out have been ignored

For many years, federal officials and educators have ignored reliable information about effective instruction in favor of "fairness." Fairness, to them, implies that every teaching method is of the same value, though some have been proven effective and some haven't. They don't want to favor one method over another, data be damned![8] Yet without data, how can we support what they say?

Here's the question: why don't we demand that in teaching children we base as many of our decisions as we can on the most reliable evidence we have?[9] Is there one good reason why we shouldn't? Why do we allow personal preference to determine the instructional programs that teachers use rather than demand evidence of their effectiveness?

Why, indeed? But we do. Cathy Watkins reviewed what happened in Project Follow Through, a Congressionally mandated experimental comparison of nine instructional approaches used in Head Start. (It was mandated in the 1960s under the Johnson administration by Public Law 90-92.) It was a well-designed comparison involving 51 sites around the country. The long and short of the comparisons is this: Direct Instruction beat all other programs resoundingly in improving children's performance in basic skills (math and reading), cognition (thinking), and affect (feeling good).[10] Did that mean that the federal government got behind Direct Instruction as a preferred model? No! What happened is a sad story that is much like what happens today. Cathy Watkins described what happened with Project Follow Through:

> The purpose of the Follow Through planned variation experiment was to identify effective educational methods. However, there is little utility in identifying effective methods if they are not then made accessible to school districts. The Joint Dissemination Review Panel [JDRP] and the National Diffusion Network [NDN] were created to validate and disseminate effective educational programs. In 1977, Follow Through sponsors submitted programs to the JDRP. "Effectiveness" was, however, broadly interpreted. For example, according to the JDRP, the positive impact of a program need not be directly related to academic achievement. In addition, a program could be judged effective if it had a positive impact on individuals

other than students. As a result, programs that had failed to improve academic achievement in Follow Through were rated as "exemplary and effective." And, once a program was validated, it was packaged and disseminated to schools through the [NDN].[11]

Ernest Boyer, then the federal commissioner of education, objected: "Since only one of the sponsors (Direct Instruction) was found to produce positive results more consistently than any of the others, it would be inappropriate and irresponsible to disseminate information on all the models . . ."[12] But Boyer's objection wasn't heeded, and I doubt any similar objection would be heeded today, and for the same reasons.

The JDRP apparently felt that to be "fair," it had to represent the multiplicity of methods in education. Not only did this practice make it virtually impossible for school districts to distinguish between effective and ineffective programs, it defeated the very purpose for which the JDRP and NDN were established!

In an article reprinted from the November 15, 1994, issue of *Newsday*, Billy Tashman summed it up this way with reference to Follow Through: "The good news is that after 26 years, nearly a billion dollars, and mountains of data, we now know which are the most effective instructional tools. The bad news is that the education world couldn't care less."[13] Not much different today, actually.

Whom do we blame for the lack of intelligent choices that Cathy Watkins and Billy Tashman describe? Tashman lays the blame on "the education world," but Watkins discusses how this world includes policy makers, colleges of education, teachers, school districts, publishers, and the public. All of us who don't make good decisions when we can—and all of us who fail to point out the lunacy of being "fair" rather than being discriminating, or knowing good from bad and best from better—bear a measure of blame. And this applies as much today as in any decades past. And it applies to special education as well as general education.

Some educators have called for scientific evidence to back up instructional techniques. That's encouraging, because among other things, it would mean getting behind DI, or at least di, direct instruction. But too often these same educators aren't serious. They say they want research-based practices, but then they waffle when push comes to shove.

Current federal involvement

The federal government now says it wants "evidence-based" education and appears to be attempting to move education toward a more scientific footing. In fact, the federal government has established an Institute of Education Sciences (IES) and a What Works Clearinghouse to promote evidence-based practices (see web addresses for these government agencies). These are encouraging developments. Yet, there are reasons for having little faith in the federal government's commitment and ability to carry through in making public education more scientific. As we've seen, once we've examined its history, federal leadership doesn't look good. The feds don't seem to be poised to do any better today, sorry to say.

Two fairly recent publications of the National Research Council on science in education contain no discussion of statistical distributions and related topics that are essential to educational research.[14] For example, they don't discuss cut points for judging proficiency or the statistical significance of a difference between means. Yet, cut points in distributions and statistical significance are essential to any rational interpretation of the federal No Child Left Behind Act policies related to achievement gaps and to judging schools to be "successful" or "failing." I find it inexplicable, not to mention extremely disappointing, that these publications don't address scientific issues that are critical in virtually every aspect of education policy. I'm sure that the authors of these publications understand statistics, so that's not the issue. Perhaps they judged the design of experiments to be more important than the actual statistics, which is understandable in some ways. But then, they omitted all discussion of single-case experimental designs that are critical in many important aspects of educational research. Puzzling. Neither the avoidance of statistical realities nor the absence of single-case experimental design inspires confidence.

Seat-of-your-pants teaching continues

The idea that there are no best practices in education, and that evidence will support any and all popular ideas about how best to teach, dies hard. The idea that no one way of teaching is better than another is alive and well. So teachers continue to teach by the seat of their pants. This idea may be a spin-off from the observation that no known method of instruction is foolproof or works every time. But this observation shouldn't be taken to mean that best practices don't exist. They do, they've been proven, and they should be followed until found

to be ineffective with a given student, in which case you adjust and follow up with the next-best practice. Instead, the argument seems to go like this: "If you can't find a method that *always* works, let educators choose whatever they like, whatever feels good to them. We don't want to endorse a method of instruction that doesn't work every time for every kid." I'm glad we don't tolerate this know-nothing, lassiez-faire attitude in other professions and trades. Surgeons, I hope, don't take this attitude. Why should educators?

Some things are actually impossible—like all children being above average or finding a teaching method that never fails. Some things are *known* to result in poor achievement—like having students explore only topics in which they have an interest or putting their education under student control. Then why promote them? Yet, many educators do just that. And seat-of-the-pants teaching accounts for a lot of education's tragicomedy.

Defense of dubious methods at the expense of effective instruction

The defense of instructional methods of dubious value and unproven outcomes is unfortunately too familiar. If not based on outright falsehoods, the evidence supporting them is often very weak. For many of these highly questionable approaches, the data are woefully insufficient, not showing much of substance. The assumption behind these dubious methods, sometimes implicit (and well hidden), sometimes shamefully explicit, is that teaching isn't and can't be made scientific in any meaningful way.

Some have argued for a more "organic" or "holistic" approach—whatever that means—and base it loosely on what is hyped as a trendy theory (like chaos). And some of us have actually suggested basing our decisions about education on scientific information—scientific in the old-fashioned but still feasible Enlightenment sense.[15]

Both the data and rational thinking support the superiority of direct instruction.[16] This has long been known about activities like sports and music. If you want kids to learn basketball, teach them the game; don't let them fumble around figuring out how to do it on their own. If you want them to play the piano, teach them directly; don't assume they'll eventually stumble onto piano technique. Instead, we waste time and money on "literacy-based" instruction, "whole language" learning, and other questionable schemes. Sometimes these fly-by-night, here-today-gone-tomorrow brainstorms are repackaged with new titles in an attempt to frame them in a more attractive (or deceptive) way, like "balanced instruction" for "whole language." But they're still founded on the same unsound, unproven ideas.

No doubt kids should be allowed to mess around sometimes, to try things out and explore their own ideas. But that's not teaching. That's playtime, letting them fool around. And it doesn't account for the fact that kids also need time to practice what they've learned and experiment with their new skills.

Creativity in a given art requires first mastering the fundamentals. True in basketball. True in music. True in architecture. True in surgery. Assuming that teachers and students should just wing it before they've even mastered the basics of direct instruction is foolhardy, and without having the foundational basics, it will yield but disastrous results under the sounds-good banner of creativity. Kids must learn the basics before they can be truly creative. And teachers must learn the basics of direct instruction before they can use it creatively and successfully.

The value of science

To find out what kind of teaching works best, we must follow the objective, replicable, publicly verifiable data associated with the Enlightenment and the natural sciences, engineering, and technology. This, the scientific method, requires testing hypotheses that can be supported or disproved by verifiable data. If a theory can't be proven false, then it isn't scientific. That's why "creation science" is an oxymoron (a self-contradiction); a creationist's belief "cannot be considered a scientific theory since it cannot be tested and proven wrong." That's why "true scientists must do everything possible to find the flaws in their own theories, to try to prove them false. Only if they do that and fail can we begin to have confidence in their hypothesis."[17] We must take the same attitude toward teaching methodologies.

The only alternative to science is to endorse random assertions that are either unsubstantiated or made by "believers" who require no proof beyond personal experience and conviction based on holy writ. Or worse, those who accept as fact the pronouncements of a political or religious authority regardless of evidence to the contrary. This nonscientific approach leaves us with one of two situations: (a) a cognitive morass in which the falsity of no statement can be determined—so again, one idea is as good as another, or (b) an authoritarian state or religion in which truth is made by fiat, whether

through religious or political leaders. Neither is compatible with my concept of human dignity; neither is going to improve education.[18]

Educational researcher Doug Carnine has observed that education will become a mature profession only when it rejects idiosyncratic knowledge for a common (scientific) knowledge based on objective verification through methods of scientific inquiry.[19] Most of us want and expect those who build or fix cars and airplanes, practice medicine, build houses, and so on to use scientific information in their practices. We should expect no less of public educators, general or special.

All educational programs must be clear about what students should know and be able to do. If these facts and skills are stated clearly, then we know what the goals of the program are, and we can measure progress with a reasonable degree of precision. If the program doesn't state what these facts and skills are but only describes a process (e.g., learning through exploration), then watch out! We'll have no way of knowing if the program is meeting its objectives. And even if the process objectives are met, the process doesn't tell us if students are acquiring the knowledge and skills they need.

Nothing is gained when students must guess what they're supposed to learn. In nearly all education programs in which students successfully learn facts and skills they need, it's through direct instruction. That is, the teacher is in control of instruction, not the student, and information is given to students before they're expected to demonstrate their learning of it. Giving students information vs. self-discovery doesn't mean the instruction is dull, or that students don't learn to apply acquired knowledge and skills to everyday problems. Neither does it mean students have no say in their education. It does mean students don't waste time and effort figuring out what they're supposed to learn. It also means students aren't allowed to learn misrules—the wrong things. If they do learn the wrong things, their learning is false, misleading, or useless.

Learning facts and skills can be—and is for most—a self-enhancing, exciting experience. And having those facts and skills at your disposal enables you to learn yet more. A point I made earlier, and made exceedingly clear, by writer E. D. Hirsch, Jr., is that we all need facts to think with. Without factual information, students' futures and learning are foreshortened. It's become popular to downsize facts into "factoids" and assume that drill kills learning and interest in it. If drill really kills, why did great musicians (like Ray Charles and Stephane Grappelli) repeatedly practice the same scales over and over—until their hands bled? Actually, I think it's important to "drill to thrill" on some things—learn them to the point that they become automatic and experience the pleasure of having them down pat. Only then can artists' improvisational and creativity talents be summoned.

We want educators to know lots about their subject matter but also how to teach it to kids. We want them to know lots about teaching because we don't want them to drive us or our kids crazy with their incompetence as teachers.

Let's get behind direct instruction

So step by step, what is direct instruction? This book isn't designed to be a how-to-do-it manual, but the basic idea is simple—teach the facts and skills you want the kids to learn. Have clear goals about what you want students to learn. Teach skills directly and explicitly. Teach them in small steps or increments. Don't assume that somehow students will just "discover" things or "unfold" or learn in an "authentic" way rather than through being taught directly what something means, what it is, what it does, and how to do it. And, if you explore the whole issue of instructing students directly in what you want them to learn, you will find that some people talk about direct instruction as a generic idea and some about Direct Instruction (DI, the capital letters letting you know that this is a field-tested program, not a general idea).

If you want to know more about direct instruction (or, more specifically, DI), you might get the book about it by Nancy Marchand-Martella, Timothy Slocum, and Ronald Martella, or books by Doug Carnine, Jerry Silbert, Ed Kame'enui, and Sara Tarver about using DI to teach reading.[20] You could also buy a book about successful teaching by Barbara Bateman.[21] You might do a web search for Direct Instruction or use Association for Direct Instruction as your search term.[22] Enough is enough; demand Direct Instruction! *Especially* if you are the parent of an exceptional child.

Notes for Chapter Nine

[1] For example, Bateman (2004), Engelmann (1997), Forness (2001), Forness, Kavale, Blum, & Lloyd (1997), Hirsch (1996), Lloyd, Forness, & Kavale (1998), Morris & Mather (2008), Rosenshine (1997, 2008)

[2] See Rosenshine (2008) for a fuller explanation of di or systematic instruction

[3] See Carnine, Silbert, Kame'enui, & Tarver (2005, 2010) for a description of using DI in reading

[4] Finn, Rotherham, & Hokanson (2001, p. 344)

[5] Brock, Marshall, & Tucker (2009)

[6] See Kauffman, Mostert, Trent, & Pullen (2006), Kauffman & Brigham (2009), Walker, Ramsey, & Gresham (2004)

[7] Hirsch (1996), Ravitch (2000)

[8] See Watkins (1996)

[9] Carnine (2000), Kauffman (1999, 2002)

[10] For elaboration see Engelmann (1997), Becker & Gersten (2001), Watkins (1996)

[11] Watkins (1996, p. 61)

[12] Watkins (1996, p. 61)

[13] Tashman (1996, p. 67)

[14] Shavelson & Towne (2002), Towne, Wise, & Winters (2004)

[15] See Lloyd & Hallahan (2007), Sasso (2007)

[16] Engelmann, Bateman, & Lloyd (2007)

[17] Ehrlich (2001, p. B3); see also Gould (1996, 1997a, 1997b, 2000), Shermer (1997, 2001)

[18] See Kauffman & Sasso (2006a, 2006b)

[19] Carnine (1993, 1998)

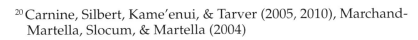

[20] Carnine, Silbert, Kame'enui, & Tarver (2005, 2010), Marchand-Martella, Slocum, & Martella (2004)

[21] Bateman (2004)

[22] See websites listed after references

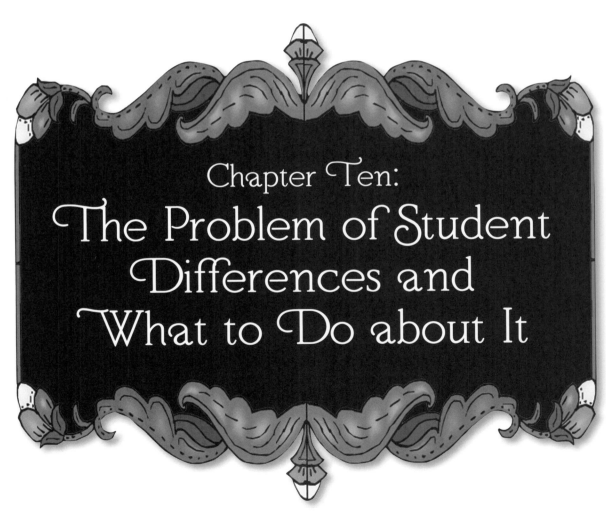

Chapter Ten:
The Problem of Student Differences and What to Do about It

How We Can Group Students Most Effectively for Instruction

One major problem in public education comes from the broad spectrum of differences we find in the students themselves. Students differ in countless ways: in their ability to grasp particular subject matter, in their skill sets (innate and learned), and in their behaviors and personalities. They come from wildly different backgrounds, ethnically, economically, culturally. Furthermore, responses to these differences are themselves extremely controversial. Differences among students and responses to them are a big part of the stuff of special education and of its many controversies. *Want the best teaching possible? Then educators should group students by what they know about the subject matter being learned.*

Students' experiential backgrounds also include prior teaching and learning. Hardly anyone who comments on education believes such differences don't exist. In fact, individual differences are recognized by most people as a reality. People differ on so many factors, such as their interests, attitudes, and motivation, that it's difficult to identify *in*variant (nondiffering) characteristics.[1] So the question, really, is what we should do about this reality of differences among students in what they know and can do. Here's the deal: *the most effective teaching can occur only when students are grouped homogeneously according to the skills they already have in what's being taught.*

If you've tried teaching, you've encountered differences

If you've tried your hand at teaching in a public school—in fact, if you've been a teacher of any sizeable group of children in *any* situation—you'll know something about the diversity of experiences, abilities, and interests that teachers face. Never mind the usual use of the word "diversity" to signify differences in color, gender, ethnicity, religion, culture, or any other personal characteristic that doesn't determine a student's abilities, interests, and experiences. Our concern here is the differences or diversities most relevant to teaching and learning. Research doesn't suggest that such things as skin color, ethnicity, gender, and religion determine how a child is best taught or how a child best learns.[2] All children, regardless of these *educationally* trivial differences that loom so large to many people—color, gender, ethnicity, culture, and so on—learn in very much the same way. Yes, we should recognize and honor such differences, but no they don't have much, if anything, to do with effective instruction.

Differences related to effective instruction

Education isn't something you can just hand out. It requires not only the presentation of something—what the teacher offers—but a response by the student. Students aren't objects that can be processed into some standard product or manufactured to a uniform tolerance. The output of education is going to be at least as varied as the input—that is, differences that we see in the early years of schooling aren't going to disappear. In fact, the better the education, the more varied the output is likely to be. That is, the differences in learning among children (the *variance or variability*, in the parlance of researchers) are going to be increased more by good education than by poor education. Good education won't homogenize a group; it will make it more diverse or heterogeneous in what students know and can do.

Students, like all of us, differ in the rate or speed with which they pick things up. Some are very fast learners. The fastest are usually considered gifted. Some are very slow learners. The slowest are usually considered to have an intellectual or developmental disability—the latest terminology for the more familiar concept of mental retardation. So just consider what happens over time when things differ in speed. What happens is that they get farther apart as time goes on. For example, if cars or horses or human runners or anything else start at the same point and travel the same course but travel at different speeds, they get more spread out, more diverse in where they are at any given instant. The differences in their progress through the course become greater the longer we let them go. If they change the rate at which they're traveling or if they change course, particularly if they backtrack, then the relative distances among them may change, too. In fact, differences may then shrink. Same thing happens in education.

Another important observation about students is that there are often very substantial differences in a given student's abilities, interests, and experiences with particular subjects or skills to be taught. Like the rest of us, students have particular strengths and weaknesses. A given student (let's assume a male student) might be very strong in math compared to his abilities and interests in other areas of the curriculum and also in comparison to other kids his age but comparatively weak in reading. So it's important to consider differences within the same student (*intraindividual differences,* in the terminology of psychology) as well as variations among individuals.

Still another important thing to note about differences is that students differ widely in the number of areas in which their performance is way ahead or way behind that of most other kids their age. Students also differ a lot in the number of areas of their own relative strength or weakness. All of this is to say that the statistical realities about distributions apply to differences among kids in every way you can think of. Frankly, there are kids who aren't really very good compared to most others at much of anything that can be taught. There are kids who are really good at a whole lot of things, nearly everything that can be taught. Most of us are about average in our abilities to learn and to do most things. And some kids are really gifted at particular things and just awful at others. So the best thinking about characteristics like giftedness and mental retardation is that individuals should be considered gifted or retarded at specific things or in specific ways—always with reference to particular curriculum content or specific skills.[3] This in no way denies the fact that some kids are gifted at many things and some are retarded in many ways.

The implications of these observations for kids' educational progress might be clear to you. Students can and sometimes do vary their rate of progress. Sometimes teachers can successfully broaden or enrich fast learners' progress so that they don't get so far ahead in the standard curriculum. Sometimes teachers can successfully speed up a student's rate of learning so that there's a catch-up effect. But human variation in rate of learning is so great that no technique and no teacher can completely avoid the basic effect of differences in rate of learning.

What to do about variation (differences) in students

The question is, of course, what to do about this variation—how to respond to it in the best way. There are two basic ideas about what to do: first, group students regardless of differences, ensuring, in fact, that disparities are great; second, group by rate of learning to lessen the differences in the group. These are called (1) *heterogeneous grouping*, which means having "natural" groups of mixed ability or even deliberately grouping kids together with extremely different rates of learning; and (2) *homogeneous grouping*, which doesn't eliminate differences altogether but does deliberately restrict the range of differences.

Heterogeneous versus homogeneous grouping has become one of the most heated controversies in public education, general and special.

Some people think that heterogeneous grouping is the better choice because kids have to learn how to cope with others who learn faster or slower than they do and because students who are slower will be taught by those who are faster. Other people think homogeneous grouping is better because students can be taught more efficiently that way and because students enjoy education more when it's appropriate for them. Following are some observations that I and my colleagues have made about this controversy.[4]

Students don't have much fun and don't learn much when they know very little or nothing about the subject at the level it's being taught or can't do what's expected. Furthermore, when students are in classrooms in which they're not really tuned in to the material or capable of doing the work, then they're likely to do whatever is required to escape—like adults under similar circumstances, they just want out of there. If the instruction is too difficult, requiring understanding or ability that students don't have, then they're probably going to be embarrassed, anxious, disruptive, inattentive, hostile, intimidated, all of the above, or otherwise difficult to teach. Alternatively, they will just tune out. If the instruction is too easy for them or just a review of what they already know or have mastered, then they're very likely to be bored, inattentive, and resentful.

Neither students nor classes nor teachers are very likely to have much fun when instruction and learning are poorly matched. This is why beginning musicians don't have much fun playing with an accomplished group of musicians and why accomplished athletes in any sport don't have much fun playing the game with unskilled players. Those who suggest that students who haven't mastered academic material ought to be placed for instruction with other kids their age who are more advanced might consider how they would feel if they were handed an instrument they didn't know how to play, put on stage with an accomplished orchestra, and told to play—or, at least, to *pretend* to play. True, an orchestra has many players, and any player may play a major or a minor part in a given composition. Regardless of how minor a person's part may be, that person's incompetence botches the performance.

Nonetheless, some educators recommend what amounts to a nightmare for a person of any age who's aware of others' expectations and wants to do a good job. It's easy for adults to forget the embarrassment that kids feel when they're not able to perform a minor skill. And many kids are humiliated by being put on the spot and having to demonstrate over and over their incompetence for everyone in the class to see.

I don't think this is kind in any way. In fact, I think it's awful. It's psychological torture!

Many of us have had bad dreams in which we're expected to do something that we simply can't do. Making this kind of bad dream into a reality for kids isn't a good idea. Sometimes, it's foisted on kids with the best of intentions, but it isn't the best and certainly not the only choice. Heterogeneous grouping is often promoted as a means to achieving social justice, but too frequently it ends up cheating students out of the best instruction they could have. That's not social justice. Let's consider more about what we know on the topic of grouping students for instruction.

Further consideration of grouping options

Among the options for grouping is whole-class or whole-group instruction, which necessarily means teaching a heterogeneous group. The larger the group, the more heterogeneous it's likely to be. Statistical probabilities tell us that as the group gets larger, the greater the chances of outliers—students way ahead or way behind. Of course, you could have a large group that's been selected specifically to be homogeneous—all achieving at about the same level of instruction. Another option is small group instruction, and the small group could be a same- or mixed-ability bunch. The smaller the group, the more homogeneous it *can* be. A smaller group has a lower chance of having a statistical outlier, and it can be selected to include only students on the same level. A teacher could team up learning pairs or partners closely matched in ability. Then there's always one-on-one instruction.

Undoubtedly each instructional arrangement provides some benefit to *some* students. But even with limited research to guide teachers in making decisions about groups, two elements seem critical: instructional match and flexibility in grouping. Both aspects of effective teaching—matching instruction to the group and changing groups as appropriate—require teachers to pay careful attention to how their pupils are doing. For a teacher to have a good instructional fit, she must match her lessons to assessments of student skills and present them at a pace that allows students to keep up. In fact, the teacher has to make *frequent* assessments to make modifications in instruction and materials as required.

Let's look at this a different way. You can't have good grouping without ongoing assessment. When students progress faster than their peers, the teacher must have the flexibility to move them into a more advanced group. Conversely, when students struggle to master concepts, the effective teacher assigns them to a slower group to best meet their needs.

Flexible grouping vs. tracking

Homogeneous grouping always raises the specter of tracking. And tracking, in which students proceed through their education on a rigid academic path leading to a predetermined outcome like a trade or college, has been seen as incompatible with American ideals. Nonetheless, *flexible* instructional groups do allow a teacher to match instruction to ability-specific grouping and avoid what critics call pigeonholing. That is, the teacher is able to group students by the skills they need to learn (as indicated by assessment) and then can progress at optimal speed in teaching them. Unfortunately, homogeneous grouping has gotten an undeserved bad name from the sad history of rigid, inflexible instructional groups, in which students were tracked for a year or longer with no possibility of changing groups. For example, teachers who had *redbird* or *bluebird* reading groups—formed from a single assessment done at the beginning of the school year that couldn't be corrected even when necessary—set horrible precedents for which we're still paying a price. The good news is that we know today that fluid, flexible instructional groups are consistent with good teaching practice.[5] The bad news is that it's an option still too seldom pursued. Consider this, too: grouping kids homogeneously for *instruction* doesn't mean that they can't be in heterogeneous groups for other activities. In fact, heterogeneous grouping for *noninstructional* activities is a very good idea. But when you want kids to learn specific things, logic and evidence are on the side of homogeneous grouping.

Instructional grouping is controversial, even without considering students with disabilities. But disabilities add to the diversity of students with which a teacher has to contend. What has become known as "full inclusion"—all students educated together, regardless of their abilities—ignores what we know about how students learn best and what teachers can manage.[6] Perhaps some people are willing to sacrifice children on the ideological altar of inclusion, pretending that children won't notice differences in ability to understand and perform or that, unlike adults, they will welcome diversity regardless of its nature.

Inclusion and teaching

The inclusion issue deserves more attention because it has become one of the central issues in public education. Some people argue endlessly, even about wording, taking great offense at a word they consider not sufficiently politically correct. Among some of my special education colleagues, there is even serious contention whether "general" or "regular" should be used to describe the classrooms most students attend.

The controversy about inclusion goes on primarily because some special educators insist that the general classroom is the one and only place that students should be taught. These people argue that students with disabilities shouldn't be "pulled out" of the regular classroom for special instruction for any reason. But as I understand the law, it isn't on their side. The federal special education law that was passed in 1975—and even the most recent reauthorization of that law, the Individuals with Disabilities Education Improvement Act of 2004, usually called IDEA—requires placement of students with disabilities in the *least restrictive environment* (LRE) selected from a full *continuum of alternative placements* (CAP).

The CAP ranges from full-time placement in the regular class to a variety of pull-out options. An example of a placement alternative other than full inclusion is that a student might spend some of the school day in a regular classroom but be pulled out for instruction in a special *resource room* for part of the school day. In the resource room, a special education teacher provides special instruction, usually in a small group of other students with similar disabilities. The amount of time the student spends in the resource room varies according to the judgment of the people involved in the student's education (usually teachers, psychologists, and parents). Another alternative is placement in a *self-contained* classroom for students with similar disabilities. A special, self-contained classroom is usually dedicated to full-time education of students with disabilities, although they sometimes leave the room for inclusion in a regular class for a particular academic subject. Other placement options include special schools, hospital schools, and instruction at home. The idea of the law is that schools must offer a CAP—a full array or continuum of approved options.

However, some special educators believe that the LRE provision of the law dominates the CAP and that *any* alternative to full-time regular classroom placement constitutes "segregation." That is, they tout the benefits of "full inclusion" and reject any alternative. They don't think a CAP is appropriate because the regular classroom is the LRE for *all* students—and, therefore, it's the only acceptable choice for *any* student. Bluntly, they don't like the law and think we should disobey it.

Now, just suppose you're a teacher or a kid or a parent. Do you really think the regular classroom is best regardless of a student's disruption of the class, regardless of the student's knowledge, regardless of anything whatsoever? I will ask you later to think about an example, but for now just let possible scenarios run through your mind. They aren't all pretty scenes for me, whether I take the role of parent (of a student with or without a disability), teacher (of general or special education), or student (with or without a disability).

No special educator I know argues against *all* inclusion. However, some of us do argue against the idea of *full* inclusion—meaning that it's the only game in town and no alternative is acceptable. We should be ashamed if we care more about *what* class *placement* a student gets rather than *what* that student *learns*. The idea that *where* is more important than *what* when it comes to education is simply appalling. It's a pretense of caring about what really counts for kids' futures. And it implies not so subtly that students with disabilities have only a superficial difference when it comes to their education, yet one that is educationally the equivalent of color or culture. This simply doesn't stand up to a logical or a legal analysis of these differences much less speak to their meaning as a civil rights issue.[7]

We need to find out more about this. As Mark Twain said, "It is wiser to find out than to suppose."[8] This maxim applies not just to the scientific principle, but to the problem of teaching all children together, regardless of differences. Otherwise, we're just pretending that we know what works best, and our pretense leaves children tricked, not taught. But, of course, we also need to use our powers of reason to try to figure out what's likely to be best, based on the research and field-test data we already have.

Experience and reason in grouping

My experience and the analysis of the problem of teaching children with diverse characteristics, as well as the data, do *not* suggest that all children can be taught well in either random or purposefully heterogeneous (inclusive) groups. Teachers are extremely unlikely to be able to teach *all*, or even *most*, children well when the class is extremely diverse. Researcher Naomi Zigmond, who has long questioned the logic of full inclusion, wrote, "General education settings are best

for learning what most students need to learn."[9] Therein lies the rub, since those with disabilities are by definition not "most students" and require a very different instructional protocol from that of most. This is generally so because they're often not "getting" what the other, more typical students are being taught and need a modified (special) approach. And even when they're learning the same things, it's often at a much slower rate than that of typical peers with whom they share inclusion classes. These disconnects—slower or little or no learning—often are intimidating, uncomfortable, and counterproductive for students with disabilities. We have to ask ourselves, "Is realizing the ideal of full inclusion worth that price?"

Having said this, we must boldly state that for many students with disabilities, the best instructional environment will not be the general education classroom. Without question, *some* students with disabilities can and do need to learn the same things at the same rate as most students and *should* be included in regular classes. But we mustn't extrapolate from *some* to *all*. That is a dangerous leap of faith, not proven in the data or in the experiences of many dedicated master teachers. Other teachers who are equally accomplished have simply been hornswoggled by what is in essence a faith-based belief system, presented as a civil rights issue, but entirely without verifying data. Let's be clear that decisions must be made about student placements—*by law*—on a case-by-case basis.[10] Sweeping decisions about inclusion that apply to every student with disabilities are not only logically wrong but legally wrong. And make no mistake about this: teaching students with disabilities in addition to more typical students increases the difficulty of the regular teacher's task. Furthermore, the more students the teacher has and the more diverse the group of students in what they need to be taught, the more difficult the job for all teachers, general or special.

Public education, at least its K–12 part, has very little or no control of the students brought to it. What it does have, to a large extent, is control over how students are grouped for instruction. Fundamentally, few educators can argue against the notion of meeting students where they are—that is, teaching them on their level. Providing instruction at the right level is obviously beneficial to students. But some educators will suggest *differentiated* instruction, which means trying to meet the instructional needs of *all* students in the class by making different kinds of assignments and having different expectations for different kids.[11] Although differentiation, within limits, is not only possible but characteristic of good education, I wonder this: how can a teacher differentiate enough to accommodate the needs of *all* students in a heterogeneous group, regardless of their level of learning? And is there a teacher alive who's working in today's overcrowded and wildly diverse classrooms who has that kind of prep time? Realize that here we're essentially talking about having to write three or more sets of lesson plans, drills, tests, etc., for a single classroom, instead of just one.

What can I say? Neither my experience or observations in schools nor a logical analysis of the problem nor any research I know of suggests this is a reasonable or responsible option. As scholar and researcher Michael Gerber has pointed out, a careful analysis of the economics of teacher time and effort suggest this is nothing more than pie-in-the-sky thinking.[12] Teachers simply can't, as a matter of practice and as shown by mathematical analyses, achieve maximum performance from students who differ greatly in learning if they must teach them at the same time. This is all so transparently obvious, one can only shrug hopelessly at the need to state it. Bottom line: because of this, too often students with disabilities as well as the gifted get lost in the shuffle.

NCLB and grouping

The No Child Left Behind Act (NCLB) could be seen as an attempt to improve the instruction of all students.[13] That laudable goal requires educators to consider how diverse groups of students can be taught best. This includes students with disabilities, not just students differing in color, ethnicity, gender, wealth, or other characteristics that don't determine what a student knows or can learn. The goals of teaching all children well and teaching all children in the same place and at the same time, though, are on a collision course when students with disabilities or gifted students are considered. The train wreck of these two goals—teaching all students well *and* in the same place and time— is unavoidable unless, in some cases and when necessary, we have the flexibility to give up one for the other. *Some* students with disabilities and *some* gifted students can be and are taught very well in regular classrooms, but this simply isn't *always* possible.

Whenever we hear or read that "all children will . . .," we should start thinking what this means. If *all* is taken literally, then the statement is clearly detached from the real world. If *all* means most (but not all), then the statement might be plausible. If *all* means each of the students in a carefully preselected group, then the statement is probably believable. Unfortunately, *all children* is often taken literally and becomes part of a silly expectation, something not grounded in reality.[14]

When an *all-or-nothing* standard of performance is added to the literal interpretation of *all children*, the silliness is compounded. Anybody who suggests that literally "*all* students will _____" (be proficient or not be graduated or passed to the next grade unless they meet this expectation) is either (1) setting up students for predictable failure and parents for outrage, or (2) referring to all students in a preselected group. When we have higher standards, high-stakes testing, and all-inclusiveness, then the following newspaper headline is predictable: "All-or-nothing tests causing states' grief."[15]

The instructional folly of teaching all students together

I think that all sentient children can and should be taught well, regardless of what they've learned. However, not all children of any given age have learned the same things, so they can't all be taught in the same setting, much less learn the same things at the same time. Good teaching is geared to prior learning. A hallmark of poor teaching is instruction that *isn't* attuned to students' understanding and ability to perform. We've known this for many decades. It's not a new insight or a new research finding. Furthermore, this basic principle is as true for reading, math, science, and other academic subjects as it is for music, sports, and other activities.

People who maintain that all students of the same age, regardless of what they know or can do, must always be taught together are just living in la-la land, in my opinion. True, there are certain things like color and parentage and sex and money that are absolutely irrelevant for teaching and learning and should not determine the school or instructional group in which a student is taught. But the suggestion that what a student knows, what a student can do, and what a student needs to learn—instructionally relevant characteristics—shouldn't determine a student's inclusion in a school or class . . . is just plain irrational. I've already explained why. But, if you need more information, go to the writings of educators Siegfried Engelmann, Bonnie Grossen, and Naomi Zigmond.[16]

I've heard and read, mostly from colleagues, that we should stop saying of students who don't know or can't do specific things that they have deficits and therefore need remediation. These people seem to think that if we say students have deficits, we're condemning them with a "deficit model." They suggest that these kids should be treated like everyone else or be seen as just part of the normal variation in the population. They've written these things even about students with identified disabilities! To me, this is like saying that we don't want to say that sick kids have health problems or need treatment, that obese children carry extra pounds and need to lose weight, that youngsters who are depressed have thought processes that need correction, and so on. It's a form of denial that does nothing to help kids, that works against their best interests, and only serves to allow these adults to feel smug that by not passing judgment they take the higher ground. But, passing sensible judgments (such as accurate diagnoses) that help to remediate kids' problems is exactly what responsible adults should be doing. In my opinion, it's better to recognize the reality that when kids do have deficits they need remediation. It's better not just to think this but to be willing to talk about it and provide the help needed. While it does, indeed, put kids in a special group of those who need special help, that's part of the schools' mission: to recognize those kids who are in a group needing special help and provide it for them.

What a teacher might face in heterogeneous grouping

If you're not yet convinced, consider an example: suppose a fourth-grader can't read the grade level math text and materials, can't solve math problems, and has yet to master second-grade reading or math concepts and operations. Some educators will suggest—seriously, this is no joke or exaggeration!—having this student participate in a fourth-grade math class with various "supports" such as peer-tutoring, cooperative learning, and other trendy tricks of the trade. They will argue that the student will pick up valuable content-related knowledge informally or incidentally by participating in this class, not to mention the invaluable socialization of having this student work and interact with age peers. They might also say that teachers, like everyone else, are expected to be able to multitask, meeting the diverse needs of all students at once through some sort of vague but unfailing "differentiated" instruction.

The literature and my own observations in schools lead to a different conclusion. We know that *some* teachers are capable of teaching *some* students with different educational needs within the context of a regular classroom and curriculum. But there simply isn't any evidence that *all* teachers are capable of teaching *all* students effectively or even that *some* teachers are capable of teaching *all* students effectively. To reach that conclusion—that a teacher can teach *all* students well, regardless of their learning characteristics—is just a matter of faith or

ideology.[17] If you're the parent of an exceptional child or of a typical child, you have a right, indeed a duty, to be skeptical of the claim that *all* children can be taught best in the same place at the same time.

Maybe some truly unusual, heroic teachers can manage incredible diversity; they can survive and stay ahead of the curve with long hours of planning and tremendous cooperation and support from co-teachers, paraprofessionals, and administrators. They might plan elaborate grouping arrangements and activities that allow them to target the student who is learning to count as well as the student who is solving algebra problems. But besides their own mental and physical health, there are questions about the effects of this heroic effort on the quality of the educational experiences for all of the students in the class. Are these teachers really challenging the advanced students in the class? Gifted students need to be challenged by the work their teacher gives them. They also need the challenge of learning with other students who are on about the same level and can give them a run for their money in figuring things out.

So, even of the unusual, heroic teachers, we have to ask, "Are these teachers really providing the best instruction for students who are gifted *and* those who are struggling or unable to cope with the instruction that is right for more typical students?" Students with disabilities are entitled to focused, intensive instruction on their level. So are gifted students. Anyone might reasonably have grave doubts about these heroic teachers—what they are doing to themselves and what they are doing for their students. They could be working harder at inclusion than they are at appropriate instruction, and that would not be a good use of their talents.[18]

Let's group kids homogeneously for best instruction

Effective instruction in *any* school depends on a school-wide commitment to *instructional grouping based on skill level*. Only then can all students, regardless of their ability, receive instruction that is just right *for them,* neither frustrating nor boring for them. Without attention to appropriate grouping, instruction becomes patronizing. But, of course, this means that not all students will be included in all instructional groups. This is awful only for people who care more about image or ideology than they do about instruction. And I think this sells kids short.

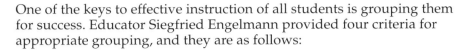

One of the keys to effective instruction of all students is grouping them for success. Educator Siegfried Engelmann provided four criteria for appropriate grouping, and they are as follows:

1. The child's performance should be 70 percent correct the first time on the material that is being taught.

2. The child should be at least 90 percent correct the first time on material that's been taught previously and is assumed to have been mastered.

3. The child should be able to go through a lesson in the anticipated amount of time and should not require great amounts of additional practice.

4. At the end of each lesson, the child should be virtually 100 percent correct on everything present in the lesson.[19]

You can't get this kind of grouping if you just assign students to the same class regardless of what they've learned. The fact is that appropriate grouping—dealing with differences among students by grouping them for instruction by what they know or can do—is a hallmark of effective instruction.[20]

If we really want schools in which *all* children learn well, then it's clear to me that homogeneous grouping for instruction in particular subject matter is essential. Refusing to create and maintain a diversity of relatively homogeneous groups is, ultimately, refusing to recognize and accommodate the diversity of students' instructional needs.[21] If we assume that the diversity of children's learning characteristics is good but that diversity in *where* they learn it or *who they learn it with* is more important than what they learn, then we embrace the opposite of what we say we want children to learn—logical thinking and compassion for others.

Notes for Chapter Ten

[1] Kauffman & Konold (2007), Konold & Kauffman (2009)

[2] Kauffman, Conroy, Gardner, & Oswald (2008)

[3] Hallahan, Kauffman, & Pullen (2009)

[4] Kauffman, Landrum, Mock, Sayeski, & Sayeski (2005), Kauffman, Mock, Tankersley, & Landrum (2008)

[5] See, for example, Vaughn, Hughes, Moody, & Elbaum (2001)

[6] Kauffman & Hallahan (2005a, 2005b), Kauffman (2003a), Kauffman & Hung (2009), Warnock (2005), Zigmond (2003), Zigmond, Kloo, & Volonino (2009)

[7] Kauffman & Landrum (2009b)

[8] Library of America (1976, p. 943)

[9] Zigmond (2003, p. 197)

[10] Bateman & Linden (2006), Hallahan et al. (2009), Huefner (2006), Kauffman & Hallahan (2005a)

[11] Hallahan et al. (2009)

[12] Gerber (2005); see also Zigmond, Kloo, & Volonino (2009)

[13] Mathews (2003)

[14] See Kauffman (2002), Kauffman & Hallahan (2005a, 2005b)

[15] *Charlottesville Daily Progress* (2003, p. B1)

[16] See Engelmann (1997), Grossen, (1993), and Zigmond (2003, 2007, 2009); see also Gallagher (1993), Gamoran (1992)

[17] For example, see Baker & Zigmond (1995), Grossen (1993), Engelmann (1997), MacMillan, Gresham, & Forness (1996), Zigmond (1997, 2003)

[18] See Mock & Kauffman (2002, 2005)

[19] Engelmann (1997, p. 183)

[20] Engelmann (1997), Becker & Gersten (2001)

[21] Kauffman & Hallahan (1997, 2005a)

Part II
Thinking and Fixing

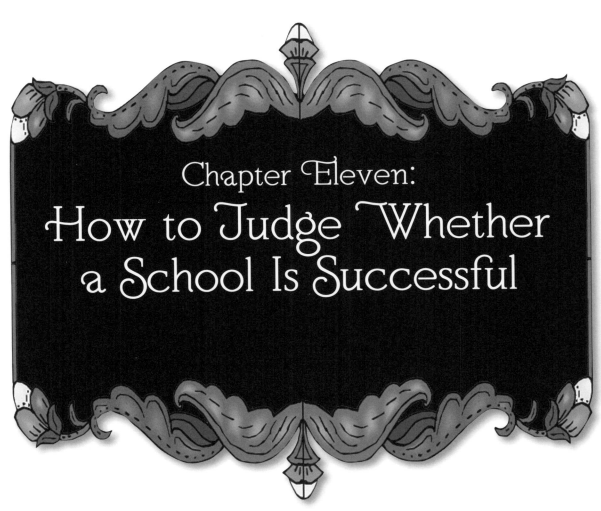

Chapter Eleven:
How to Judge Whether a School Is Successful

How Better Judgment about Successful Schools Can Spur On Improvement

Much is made these days about failing vs. successful schools and the freedom of parents to choose a thriving school if theirs is lacking. Schools have always been a concern, but the No Child Left Behind (NCLB) and the school reform rhetoric of the early twenty-first century have cast a powerful new spotlight on school successes and failures with an unfortunate emphasis on consequences for the latter. Regrettably, as has been noted in many critiques, NCLB and the forbidding scales with which it weighs success vs. failure are only concerned with test scores. No other criterion is figured in. And the tragedy is that a school is judged solely by whether it meets criteria that are utterly intellectually bankrupt.[1] *Judging schools' success by the average test scores of various groups is crack-brained.*

The NCLB view of successful schools is particularly noxious in the case of special education. In part, this is because NCLB achievement expectations are unreasonable. Far worse, though, it's because these school failures scapegoat kids with disabilities, who when the school is found to be lacking are blamed as a group that was unable to meet the mean and thus brought their school down because of *their* failures. *Successful schools provide good instruction, engage students in productive activity, have a positive emotional climate, have school-wide expectations and consequences, focus on support of positive behavior, and earn the approval of parents; and they support students and families, regardless of students' level of performance.* This is a far cry from the goals of NCLB, but it's a view of success grounded in what schools are for.

The lunacy of NCLB criteria for successful and failing schools

Think about what NCLB says about success criteria: that eliminating gaps in performance between students with disabilities and others must be accomplished. This is ludicrous—unrealistic to put it too mildly. Part of the definition of a school-related disability is precisely the idea that the student can't meet the standards appropriate for other students *because of the disability.* Therefore, the idea of doing away with the gap in average academic achievement test scores between students with and without disabilities represents either grotesque misunderstanding or outright denial. True, we want students with

disabilities to learn all they can. True also that through persistent hard work some will overcome enormous odds.[2] But NCLB focuses on group averages, not on individuals. The Individuals with Disabilities Education Act (IDEA), the federal education law having to do specifically with disabilities, wisely focuses on the individual, not the group.[3] The *average* for students with disabilities will never match that of those without disabilities, regardless of individual gains and accomplishments. We know this about disabilities.[4] So when it comes to students with disabilities as a group, NCLB is really off the wall in its basic assumptions. School psychologists Misty Ginicola and Christina Saccoccio have pointed out that the unintended consequences of NCLB aren't just unreachable standards or expectations but a threat to children's mental health.[5]

The thought that all schools, like all students, will meet some specified test criterion flies in the face of what we know about statistical realities—unless the criterion is set at zero. So much for critical thinking. Those very people who want students to be able to think critically about important issues have themselves failed to do just that when it comes to NCLB and related laws! They don't seem to have taken into consideration basic mathematics. It's like a conspiracy of denial and ignorance, including politicians and business executives, not just "educationists." If that isn't tragicomic, what is? Their standard for identifying successful schools is so out in left field it suggests smug solutions for big problems based on nothing more than fantasy.

Still, a reasonable, nagging question remains: what defines a successful school? The opposite question puzzles us as well: what defines a failing school? It's okay to criticize criteria as silly or irrational, but only when serious and rational criteria are offered in their place.

Alternatives to NCLB for judging schools' success and failure

The bad news is that only some schools can be successful *if* the criteria are based on comparisons among schools or *if* the judgment is based on students meeting a specified test criterion (which, of course, requires comparing a school's average test scores to a statistical distribution). This applies equally to *any* outcome or criterion when it alone determines success. Given the realities of mathematics, statistics, and test scores, it's a given that if meeting a certain comparative standard of students' test scores is the way we define success and failure, then some schools will *have* to be judged failures. When set criteria for success *guarantee* these failures, we might wonder about the wisdom and the objectives of such criteria. Are we paranoid when this makes us wonder if the idea is to rid ourselves of public education altogether (that is, loading the deck against it, then making the case for its failure)?

The good news is that there are rational ways to judge school performance in which *every* school *could* be said to be successful. Note, I'm not arguing that if a school has failed, it shouldn't be seen as failing and rehabilitated. It should. And by the same token, the criteria to which I'm referring also allow the possibility that *every* school could be called a failure. Every policy maker interested in promoting successful public schools needs to ask: could every school do this?

Some analogies help us think this through. It's impossible for every baseball team in the same league to have a winning season. Yet the fact that a team does poorly in its league doesn't mean it's no good. Statistically, we know that half of the teams in a given league will have a losing season. Now a team might be really good or a lot better than it was the previous season and still end up having a losing season because other teams outperformed it. Lots of exceptional athletes don't make the Olympics, much less earn a medal. We have precisely the same situation with schools when judged by student test scores. Expecting all schools to be winners by NCLB criteria leaves any rational person who thinks about it gaw-gaw.

But we could establish test criteria for sports performance and say any player or team that reaches it gets the stamp of approval. Taking the analogy further, there are two major problems. One, the criterion is still solely outcome-based. So regardless of training, practice, dedication, or motivation, what determines success or failure is the person's ability. Two, in athletic competitions the coach decides who's on the team, namely the most capable performers. Schools can't decide not to take certain students. They don't get to select their players, if players equal students. Consider this scenario: suppose everyone who lives near your gym is on the team, no exceptions for disabilities. The team isn't selected from those interested in the game or who have requisite skills. They live in a given area, so they're on the team. Fat, thin, weak, strong, interested or not, experienced or not, knowledgeable or not, you got 'em, coach. And let's say they all have to play; none of them can just stay on the bench. Now, how well do you think that team will compete?

You might be forgiven for thinking, "Whoa, this is a whole new ballgame!" The sports analogy breaks down because, unlike sports teams that can field just their best players, in public schools everybody has to play—no school is exempt, no students or groups are exempt, schools don't pick just the best students. Analogies are helpful in understanding how things work, but only when things being compared are as close to parallel as possible.

Same goes with business analogies. In public schools the "manager" of the school (the superintendent), who is the "manufacturer" of students, doesn't have any control over the raw materials she has been given to work with. We tend not to consider how difficult, even impossible, it would be for a business to maintain quality control when it has no control over its materials, by analogy students' talents. Dirty water? No excuse? Inferior grade of a given resource? No excuse. Lack of equipment? No excuse. This is your business, but you don't select your materials, your equipment, or your plant.

While we should look at a school's outputs, not just its inputs, we must also be realistic enough to look at both. Outputs are important, but they shouldn't be the *only* basis for judging a business, a team, or a school. What you have to work with is as important to consider as what you do with it. Reasonable, rational people look at both input and output. Reasonable people in a business don't waste time and effort imagining that they can make silk purses from sow's ears. Nor do reasonable educators waste time and effort supposing that their students might benefit from some instructional program for which there is only shaky evidence or that they can make *all* students brilliant. In both businesses and schools, reasonable people demand inputs that they have good reason to believe are the most likely to succeed based on fair trials and reliable data. They look at how outputs (whether manufactured goods or student competencies) have been obtained using particular inputs (processes or instruction).

Understand, too, that you can't have accountability for success or failure without some form of measurement. Further, all measurements, including those we might devise for schools, produce a statistical distribution or, at least, yes-no judgments. So at one level, we can't get away from making comparisons and dealing with statistics when we judge schools. What we *can* do in business, though, is something we can't do in education. In schooling children, we're not allowed to judge some students to be unacceptable, to say that they have no right to schooling because they don't meet our expectations. But we can say of a *school*, "It doesn't meet our expectations." A school staff *is* like a team—a *selected* group of individuals chosen for their abilities and interests. This isn't like having a group of students who are selected solely on the basis of their domicile. A school staff member's selection

is ability-based, and the staff member should present proof of ability to join the team. The school simply should not hire just anyone who lives in the community, regardless of specific skills and appropriate training. Nor would you want it to.

Reasonable people know that kids differ tremendously in their learning characteristics, and they make allowances for them. They know that not all students have the same abilities and that some schools have a lot more low-ability students and some schools have the opposite. They know this is nothing more than an accident of location. They don't let this reality keep them from getting every student to perform at the highest level possible or from trying to make their school the best it can be. But neither do they assume that *all* kids can meet a given standard, especially one that applies across many schools. What's important is that all kids give learning their best effort and that all teachers give teaching their best effort while using the best, proven methods of instruction. This is a far cry from assuming that all kids will learn up to a given standard—and that if they don't, it's the teacher's or the school's fault.

Seven criteria for judging success and failure

Here's how I think we should judge a school's success: the top seven criteria—ones I think are most important. Let's elaborate on each:

1. **Instruction**—Successful schools use the instructional methods that result in the greatest number of students learning what's being taught, according to the best field tests and most reliable data.

2. **Engagement in productive activity**—Successful schools see to it that the vast majority of students' time is spent in productive learning activity, not in busy work or idleness.

3. **Grouping**—Successful schools do flexible homogeneous grouping, placing students in groups according to what they know and what they need to learn. These groups are not rigid tracks but are specific to the subject matter and change with changes in a student's performance.

4. **Climate**—Successful schools make sure they are inviting, accepting, encouraging places where students' interests and happiness are fostered and where students can count on adults showing real interest in and concern about them.

5. **School-wide expectations**—Successful schools are those in which *all* school personnel are on the same page when it comes to behavioral expectations, so that there is consistency from place to place and time to time in what is praised, what is tolerated or ignored, and what is punished and how. *All* school personnel includes nonteaching staff, too—custodians, cooks, and secretaries, for example. School-wide means that there is consensus, if not unanimous agreement, about how to respond to what kids do.

6. **Positive behavioral support**—Successful schools emphasize positive support in the form of praise and recognition for appropriate behavior and achievement, and they emphasize rewarding consequences rather than punishment or some other form of censure for undesirable conduct or performance.

7. **Parent and community involvement**—Successful schools get families and communities involved in what they're doing and make every effort to earn and deserve the enthusiastic support of the parents.

Note that for these seven characteristics, implementation of a system for measuring, or judging, each is suggested. How each criterion should be weighted and what the cut-point should be for judging success or failure is up to your good judgment. Still, I think these are reasonable criteria, the things we should be looking for—certainly far more sensible and telling than aggregate test scores of groups of students. Let's look at each of the seven criteria in more depth.

1. Good instruction

The first criterion for a successful school is instruction. You can't have a successful school when the instructional program is seriously off kilter. It's entirely possible, using outcome measures or test results alone, to have a school that has dismal instruction, while its students are on average so capable that aggregate test scores are high anyway. All you need to have for this to occur is a lousy administration in a well-heeled district where the school population is dominated by the children of highly educated professionals. When given those conditions, test scores will soar regardless, yet the fact remains that with better instruction they'd be even higher. This latter fact, that we could have done better, is the only conclusion that should concern us. Conversely, a school in a rural area may have students who weren't raised on the great books, the opera, and the theatre and have little sophistication in their

background, yet benefit from terrific instruction and have respectable or even terrific test scores. All of this makes school-wide test score comparisons enormously conditional when used as the sole criteria for success or failure.

Good instruction means kids are being taught directly what they need to learn, not just being turned loose to discover things for themselves. This does *not* mean that with good instruction kids should never be allowed to explore for themselves but that "discovery learning" should never be the focus. The focus should always be provided by direct instruction so that the object of a given lesson is clear, information is imparted expediently to students, and their responses to questions or problems arising during the lesson make it clear to the teacher what they do and don't know. Good instruction should also mean that students are always being taught at their individual instructional level, not someone else's level. This does not necessarily mean instruction on the grade level at which they're enrolled, but at a level at which they understand the material and can give a correct response at least 70 percent of the time. Studies show that when students are grouped homogeneously by their achievement level, they perform best.

2. Productive activity

In a successful school, students are engaged for the majority of their time in productive activity. Don't misunderstand; no school should have students engaged in productive activity 100 percent of the time. Everyone needs down time, even the most productive among us. But we should expect students to spend at least 70–80 percent of their time in school doing such meritorious things as paying attention, giving a response, working with focus on a project, or doing something constructive, not just fiddling away the time, waiting, watching others, doing busy work, and so on.

Casual observers often think kids *aren't* engaged in productive activity when they are. They mistakenly see disorganization or chaos when students are getting organized, working relatively noisily with others on problems, or are otherwise doing what they should be. But we also see time being wasted in school in ways that can't be justified. Usually, when that is the case, it's because students don't know what they're supposed to be doing. The teacher didn't make directions clear or didn't have a coherent plan, or the administration is so busy pushing trendy new programming that there's no prep time for academics. It's always of primary importance for students to know what the staff wants them to do. Bottom line: in a successful school, students spend most of their time, defined as a minimum of 70 percent or more, learning.

3. Homogeneous grouping for instruction

If schools are going to be as successful as possible, then they have to group students homogeneously for instruction in specific skills (and stress direct instruction in all academic areas). I dealt with this issue in detail in Chapter 10. While some educators will insist that slower students will learn a lot from those who are faster, that heterogeneous classes are best, and that instruction can be "differentiated" to meet the needs of individuals, including the special needs of students with disabilities, for the most part these arguments are just bunk. That is, homogeneous grouping for instruction is better if what we're after is the highest level of learning possible for individual students regardless of their prior learning and ability in a subject. This allows the most efficient instruction a teacher can offer. If that's not our goal, only then do arguments for heterogeneous student groupings make sense.

If you're judging whether a school is headed for success or failure, first look into how students are grouped for instruction. And know this: success is far more likely when students study and learn with others who are on roughly the same level. The larger the discrepancies among student ability levels, the higher the risk of failure.

4. Good emotional climate

Most people can tell what the emotional atmosphere of a school is when they walk into it. If you can't read the climate after spending some time in a given school, chances are it isn't a particularly safe place to be. Successful schools are places where most people are happy most of the time, where there's an instinct toward and a tradition of helping others, an encouragement of interest in learning. The feeling is one of approachability, of concern for individuals and the community, and most of all there is a positive mental attitude toward what goes on. In successful schools, if you spot people who are out of sorts, they're in the minority, and their negativity doesn't spread; their negative energies are isolated while systemic efforts are built in to get them back on track, to engage them in activities that bring out their best and make them easier to be around. In short, successful schools tend to be those about which students will say, "I like going to school here," where most employees say, "I like working here," and where you feel it's a place you'd like to be yourself.

5. School-wide expectations and consequences

The most successful schools have expectations for conduct that are school-wide. They're places in which school employees have agreed on what's successful and what isn't and know how to monitor and respond promptly to desirable and undesirable behaviors. In these schools, you won't find irreconcilable differences or disagreements between teachers about which behaviors are considered tolerable and which aren't; teachers and administrators are on the same page. Teachers in successful schools aren't surprised or exasperated by administrator or staff responses to misbehavior because everyone knows the rules, which are enforced with rigorous consistency. The staff works together to monitor students, to disseminate school-wide expectations, and to apply appropriate consequences for behavior, good and bad. The emphasis of the school is on the positive—on behavior that's good for the individual and community, and helpful to others. Constant monitoring, consistency, and emphasis on what school staff *wants* students to do contribute to a positive school climate. Consistent sanctions for bullying and other inappropriate behavior add to the feeling of safety in the school. In short, in an effective school, students are likely to be given explicit praise and approval for desirable conduct, and because they're watched carefully rather than ignored outside the classroom, problems are nipped in the bud and chances of serious misbehavior are considerably lowered.

6. Focus on positive support for desired behavior

In successful schools, educators know that some students need more behavioral help than do others. In the typical school, we find 10 percent or more who need extra help in adopting desirable conduct, and 3 to 5 percent who need intensive help to overcome serious social problems. A strong school-wide monitoring program with consistent responses to problems, including a focus on reinforcing desirable behavior, takes care of most behavior problems. But for about 10 or 15 percent, additional help is needed.

Educators understand that most behavior is learned—that most behavior problems are learning problems, that students need to learn social graces and learn what behavior is not tolerated. The best approach for dealing with problem behavior, and the one with the most extensive basis in research, is called *positive behavioral support* (PBS, sometimes called *positive behavioral intervention and support* or PBIS).[6] Its focus is on teaching and especially on consistent rewarding of positive behavior while minimizing punishment for misbehavior. Responsible positive support for behavior doesn't reject all punishment, but punitive reprisals don't lead its parade. Studies have long shown that punishments and threats, as primary means of behavior management, are both ineffective and inhumane.[7] Punishment is a favored approach for some teachers, with some parents in agreement, thinking perhaps that children's fear of punishment is the skeleton key to discipline. But there are good reasons to de-emphasize punishment and focus on the good behavior that makes for happy adults and kids. This is equally true for young children and those who are older.[8]

The big idea here is that successful schools emphasize positive support for the behavior they want, not punishment for the behavior they don't want. The appetite for revenge, for making someone else suffer physically or emotionally for doing wrong, is strong. But satisfying this urge doesn't help schools help children, and it renders schools ineffective and stultifying for them. Helping kids behave well through a focus on positive attention and consistent support for good behavior does for a school what regular exercise and good nutrition do for your health and well-being.

7. Parent and community support

Successful schools get parental support because they contribute to the success of the community by teaching its children well. The most successful schools have the most enthusiastic parental support. Typically, teachers and administrators in these schools communicate often with parents and get them involved in the school's work. These parents know what's happening to their children at school. More often than not, they get good news from school. They find the school an inviting place where their concerns are taken seriously, not blown off. Even when they've had bad past school experiences, they find little or no basis for criticism.

But support from parents and the community doesn't come automatically. It's earned, because the school offers students an optimal learning environment and communicates effectively with parents. And it goes to great lengths to explain exactly what it offers students in down-to-earth terms understood by the vast majority of parents and other community members.

What a successful school is like

How might someone judge a successful school using the previously mentioned criteria? Here's a description of what one looks like, and I hope you'll find such a school not too far from where you live. In it, when we look into any classroom, we find good instruction going on. That is, the students are receiving the kind of direct or systematic instruction that I described in Chapter 9. They're not just being turned loose to figure things out for themselves with minimal teacher involvement. The teacher is in charge and teaching in a way that helps most students learn to the best of their abilities. In our model school, students spend most of their time actively engaged in academic tasks. There aren't many kids, if any, who are idle or seem to be frittering away their time. And students are grouped into classes and grouped within classrooms with other kids who are on the same instructional level (homogeneously grouped). Very few kids, if any, look or act bored. They know what's going on and they're plugged into it. The school is a happy place for teachers and students. They like being there. The staff knows what behaviors are expected and what's acceptable and what's not. Bullying and disrespect aren't tolerated, regardless of who's on the receiving end. And when a student needs correction, it's done directly and unequivocally, but without hostility, embarrassment, or other harsh treatment. Teachers and administrators aren't looking for infractions as much as they're looking for kids who are doing the right and the expected things, for which they are frequently rewarded. If you ask parents or businesspeople about the school, the vast majority express pride and approval about what's happening there. They know what's going on, and they like it.[9]

Let's agree that a school's success will be judged by these criteria

When deciding whether your child's school is a success or a failure, start with something other than the test-score-based proficiency focus of NCLB. Here are seven questions to ask before passing or accepting the judgment of others:

1. Is my child getting good instruction?

2. Is my child engaged in productive activity most of the time in school?

3. Is my child grouped with others who are on about the same instructional level?

4. Is the climate of my child's school positive, hopeful, and supportive?

5. Does my child's school have a school-wide plan for managing behavior?

6. Does my child's school emphasize support for desirable behavior?

7. Does my child's school involve parents and the whole community?

Judging the success and failure of schools isn't easy. It requires that we think carefully about what's important for kids and that we actively observe what goes on. And it requires knowing enough about children and schools *not* to just go along with the accepted wisdom about them. Your child is exceptional? Ask those seven questions. Your child isn't exceptional? Ask the same seven questions. The issues are the same whether your child is exceptional or not.

Notes for Chapter Eleven

[1] Kauffman (2005), Kauffman & Konold (2007), Konold & Kauffman (2009); see also Ho (2008)

[2] Kauffman, McGee, & Brigham (2004)

[3] Johns (2003)

[4] Kauffman & Hallahan (2005a)

[5] Ginicola & Saccoccio (2008)

[6] See Kauffman & Brigham (2009), Lewis, Newcomer, Trussell, & Richter (2006)

[7] Landrum & Kauffman (2006)

[8] Kauffman & Brigham (2009), Kazdin (2008)

[9] See Loh (2008)

Part II
Thinking and Fixing

Chapter Twelve:
Advising Education Policy Makers

How We Can Better Advise Policy Makers about Education

Like many writers long dead, Mark Twain speaks to our present-day problems—from the grave, but nevertheless with startling clarity. He was a wit but not by any means a twit, a man of towering comic talent who thought deeply about serious things. How fitting that he would foresee today's tragicomedy of public policy in his own distant time! Just consider his long-buried comments (first published in the last 2008 issue of *The New Yorker* magazine) on the dangers of exercising our American freedom of speech. He explains that instead of saying things we believe or know to be true, we tend to say things to seek approval, especially when the truth is something others don't want to hear—that we go along to get along. He comments on the custom of making our opinions correspond to our neighbor's and looking for others' approval rather than thinking things through carefully—the custom of expressing polite agreement rather than saying something unpopular:

> This custom naturally produces another result: public opinion being born and reared on this plan, it is not opinion at all, it is merely *policy*; there is no reflection back of it, no principle, and it is entitled to no respect.[1]

Mark Twain reminds us that it's easy to go along with the crowd, to adopt the popular opinion and simply let policy be made by precedent or default because we think little and say less. He challenges us to think better and say more based on a careful analysis of the problem. How fitting for current policy concerning the education of our children!

Education policy is made by people who can be influenced. This is true whether we're talking about general or special education. This includes elected officials and political appointees at all levels—national, state, and local. *They need to hear more often from more of us—educators, parents, and concerned citizens.*

Their policies have tremendous impact on the education of children and the preparation of teachers. It's important to understand that what policy makers do reflects not only their own education and biases but what they read and what people tell them.[2] Therefore, they can and should be influenced, because the policies they make affect how teachers teach and how schools are run. Their decisions often affect

schools, teachers, and children for generations. *We need to write and speak out more if we want our schools to improve—and if we want public education to be less tragicomic than it is now.*

The fact that a law is passed, even if it was with good intentions and overwhelming bipartisan support, doesn't make it rational or defensible. Votes may tell us something about the political palatability of a policy, but they tell us nothing about whether the policy is grounded in reality. Votes don't transform the realities of a bad idea, they simply reflect a political reality. Passing a bill doesn't give it a credibility that it didn't otherwise have, any more than truth is made by what most people think. Votes tell us what people think, not what is possible or wise. But don't forget the realpolitik at work here: what's good advice for policy makers isn't necessarily the best idea but the popular notion that gets the most votes. While you may find it an uphill fight at first, that's all the more reason for engaging in the battle.

Seven suggestions for policy makers

Too much of our public education system is based on fantasy or misunderstanding. It's just foolishness that's not based on the best evidence we have or on rational thinking about that evidence. Below, my colleague, statistician Tim Konold, and I suggest seven policies for practitioners and for petitioning those who make policy decisions.[3]

1. Before you enact or support a policy, make sure it's based on all of the realities we know about education.

2. Educate yourself about education. Seek out reliable, data-based information so you have a firm basis in scientific evidence for thinking about what we know and don't know.

3. Refuse to go along with any proposal, regardless of the reasons given for it, if you believe it's inconsistent with reality.

4. Don't give in to the temptation to engage in rhetoric that doesn't conform with every known reality about education.

5. Demand that your advisors provide you with the kind of data and thinking that will convince reasonable skeptics—people who want scientific evidence as the basis for decisions.

6. Demand consideration of all statistical information, not just measures of the central tendency of distributions. You can't make good decisions based on knowledge of averages alone; you have

to know, for example, how bunched up or how spread out the distribution is and what happens to students at the extremes of high and low.

7. Be skeptical. Before adopting a new curriculum or method of instruction, make sure you obtain field-test data indicating it's effective. Don't rely solely on the sales pitches of publishers or developers of educational materials or methods or testimonial "evidence" from advocates; demand data published in peer-reviewed sources.

A policy doesn't have to be absolutely perfect before a policy maker can support it. However, supporting a policy that we *know* is not aligned with reality is in my opinion unethical. Flaws are almost always found in policies—flaws that we didn't know existed when the policy was made. In fact, many policies have unintended consequences, and we can't hold people responsible for unpredictable results.[4]

Nevertheless, in our society when people know (or should know) the negative consequences of an action but perform it anyway, we consider them negligent or malicious. As a society, we don't approve of constructing and marketing goods known to be defective. Neither do we fail to hold people responsible for negative outcomes when they should have known their actions could harm others. For example, we acknowledge that it's malicious to sell cars that manufacturers know are unsafe. Our courts generally excuse people from responsibility for things that are unknowable, but they don't excuse people from responsibility for what they knew—or even for what they *should* have known. Legally speaking, ignorance of a given law is no defense for breaking it. The education of our children, including our exceptional children, is too important to leave to the consequences of sloppy thinking about education. Bad educational decisions should be considered no less serious than manufacturing unsafe planes, trains, or cars.

Encourage better thinking of policy makers

If you're talking with policy makers about education, keep in mind the ideas I've presented in this and other chapters of this book. But remember that Rome wasn't built in a day. Education policy changes slowly. It's easy to get frustrated, to see that policy makers are making big mistakes while ignoring realities or science in favor of ideologies or religious beliefs. Yet showing your frustration by demeaning policy makers—just as with punishing children harshly—will be counterproductive in the long run. This is not to say that policy makers shouldn't be challenged, questioned directly, or held accountable for their actions. Rather, it's that being tactful allows adversaries a graceful exit and is more likely to win the day than are rudeness, trap setting, and avoidable public confrontations. Still, sometimes public confrontation can't be avoided.

You shouldn't be fooled about two things. First, finding out what really does have the best support from good field tests or rigorous research isn't easy. Every program, even those designed by ideologues or outright quacks, will *claim* to have support from research. Debunking the claim of research support for ineffective programs will require you to ask questions about methodology and express reasonable skepticism.

Such as these, for example:

- Was the research published in a peer-refereed professional journal?

- How many subjects or participants were involved, and how were they selected?

- Did other people replicate the finding at multiple sites?

- Exactly what differences were found, how big were they, and what was their statistical significance?

These questions aren't exhaustive but are important first inquiries. Generally speaking, the reliability of research findings goes up with increases in sample size, random selection or assignment, thorough peer review, multiple sites or tests, and larger differences. But none of these is fool-proof.

Second, policy makers often call ostentatiously for evidence-based practices but turn around and quietly approve programs with no such support, even with evidence that is inconsistent with scientific methods or the realities of mathematics. This is the familiar tactic of confidence men—say one thing but do another, misrepresent reality because a given program or method has achieved popularity. It's hard enough to explain tragicomic realities like a policy maker's insistence on a failed program when its failure has been well documented. It's even harder to explain why a policy maker might say we should adopt evidence-based education and then turn right around and demand that we should teach a controversial subject like intelligent design instead of evolution—to call for science, then reject it, or worse, to insist students

be presented with both real science and pseudoscience with no distinction offered between them.

Those defending an ideology will do so with great passion. They're likely to make distinctions or claims that aren't interpretable or even believable to those with a healthy skepticism, such as the difference between fact and truth, between postmodernism and poststructuralism, or the claim that great evolutionary complexity implies intelligent design. They may take a position on an issue that can't be proven wrong by data or rational argument, although that means by definition they hold an unscientific belief. They may inveigh against rationality by pointing out that it has its limits, hoping no one will notice that irrationality's lack of limits isn't in itself a recommendation for it.

In this respect, navigating the shoals of the Internet is like going through pirate-infested waters. If you use a search engine for something like "evidence-based education," you'll find reliable information but also websites that sell off-the-rack baloney. It's hard to separate the bunkum from trustworthy information. I'd advise you to do a web search for Wing Institute, for example, to obtain trustworthy information.[5] There just isn't any substitute for the hard work of seeking out information, reading widely from the most reliable sources, using your powers of reason, and maintaining a healthy skepticism.

Special education, in particular, has become tragicomic because too few people, especially those involved directly in the education of exceptional children, have done this hard work. It's apparently much easier to become enthralled with catchy phrases and pop-trendy ideas, including the belief that good intentions, enthusiasm, creativity, and conformity to the latest fad or claim will carry the day.

An educational blunder

Let's look at a typical classroom blunder that has the blessing of policy makers:

Joanne, the teacher of our third-grade daughter, Emma (identified as having a learning disability), doesn't give children much information directly. She uses what she calls "child-centered" teaching in which she expects children to learn through exploration and discovery. Joanne tells us that she gives children very little feedback on their performance and is careful not to tell any child an answer is wrong. "Kids need to figure out for themselves what's right and what's wrong," she says. Besides, she feels that there are no really wrong

answers, although she does admit that some answers might be better than others.

Joanne tells us that she doesn't believe in rewarding children for good behavior or achievement with approval or in any other way because, she believes, rewards undermine internal motivation. She says learning is its own reward, and she can only set up circumstances under which children learn naturally and teach each other. "Learning, has to be authentic," she tells us, "and I'm much more concerned about the process kids are learning than about the content. They can always get the content when they need it."

Joanne seems more interested in pupils learning to work together in groups than about their learning "mere facts." She believes that standardized tests are bad, and she thinks that higher test scores mean nothing. "In fact, higher test scores might actually mean that children are learning less!" Joanne says. As parents, we just don't understand this.

We're told that Joanne's ideas about teaching are "cutting edge" according to her professors. And the principal has firmly endorsed Joanne's teaching. It appears that her ideas aren't out in left field according to other educators or administrators. Her ideas seem "new-fangled" to us, but maybe we just don't understand.

Joanne says she's committed to reforming education through implementing her ideas about teaching and learning. But Emma has been in this school since kindergarten, and after nearly four years in this school she's still reading on a first-grade level. Still, she's considered "about average" in her class. Joanne tries to reassure us. She reminds us that children develop at different rates and there's always a wide range of levels in a class. Emma will read fine in time, she believes, "when she's ready." And then she'll learn to read at her pace, not ours. "We don't want to hurry her," she tells us. And Joanne says we shouldn't worry about what's considered "normal," because, actually, there isn't any "normal." "It'll all come together for her soon," she says. For Emma's sake, we hope she's right.

Here we see how a typical tragicomedic educator, who defends catchy phrases and ideas with her very heart and soul, plays out her beliefs in action. And we see how schools too often don't serve exceptional children well. We also see that although many of these trendy reforms are very popular, we have to ask, "In what way does that matter if they fail to help children?"[6] So the question is, "What should Emma's parents do here?"

First, it's important to recognize that Joanne is probably not a lazy or incompetent teacher, but more likely that she had been indoctrinated

by misguided educators or administrators. She may truly believe that she's doing what's best for children, and she might have been told by administrators to do it. So from her perspective as a practitioner, she's blameless—her teaching was approved by those who trained her and those who hired her. Attacking her competence isn't going to get Emma's parents very far. All they can do is suggest to Joanne, as nonthreateningly as possible, that she read some well-thought-out alternative views they'll be happy to supply. However, to do so, Emma's parents would have to search out appropriate reading materials and provide Joanne with copies (such materials are included in some of the references cited in this book). The same is likely true for the parents of students Skip and Laura described in Chapters 4 and 6 respectively. Realistically, consider that just because you give a child's teacher things to read doesn't mean she'll actually read them or that she'll read them and change her mind. Indoctrination runs deep, as it truly is a type of belief system.

More likely, Emma's parents will have a better chance of changing what happens in Joanne's classroom by focusing their efforts on policy makers at higher levels. However, recall the story about George Howard and the superintendent in Chapter 2. Bad thinking isn't exclusive to teachers. It's also infected a lot of administrators, school board members, teacher trainers, and state and national education leaders.

A teacher's struggle to improve policy

Here's a report from a frustrated special education teacher about a problem often found at the school-board level.

> I wear several hats in my school system. I'm a teacher of children with special needs in an elementary school, the mother of a son who is learning disabled and receives instruction in reading from a resource teacher, and the building representative for the local teachers association. As a building representative, I'm expected to go to the school board meetings and report to all of the teachers in my building what the board proposes. Last month, one of the board members suggested that the school system adopt a "balanced instruction" reading program and that we also hire professionals to present workshops on the "balanced instruction" method of instruction. After the board member's suggestion, I spoke about the fact that over 30% of our students are considered at risk and that we also have a lot of special education students whom special education teachers are having trouble integrating or "including" in regular classrooms.

Because of the large number of at-risk and special education pupils, their teachers hoped for a more systematic, phonics-based program. I offered to bring copies of research studies about the ineffectiveness of the balanced-instruction approach with low achieving students and special education students, and I also gave the school board the name of a leading researcher in the field who teaches in the education department at the local university. I understand from my own reading that "balanced instruction" is pretty much like what used to be called "whole language."

After I spoke, the board member who suggested the balanced instruction curriculum frowned, thanked me for my opinion, and immediately spoke to another board member, Harriet Lane. She prefers to be called "Dr." Lane. The other board member asked Dr. Lane, "What about this balanced instruction, Dr. Lane? Tell us about it."

Dr. Lane has been in the education department of the local university for over 25 years, teaches science education, hasn't published since obtaining tenure, and is a joke among students because she never seems to read a journal article. However, Dr. Lane said, "Well, reading is not my area of expertise, but I know credible people in this area, and I'll be happy to discuss this with them and get back to you."

To my dismay, balanced instruction reading was a done deal with the school board on the strength of Dr. Lane's recommendation. She reported to the board that she had contacted "the top people" in the field at several universities in the country (without naming them), and that they felt that this was an excellent program (based on what information, she didn't say). She said she knew that her niece had learned to read using a balanced instruction approach and that she'd asked her niece's teacher about it and that teacher had strongly recommended it and that was good enough for her. When I asked Dr. Lane if she would tell us whom she contacted or if she could give us the published sources of her information, she frowned at me and asked, "Are you doubting my integrity?" The whole board laughed as if she'd said something very funny.

I just sat down, then. I wanted to tell Dr. Lane that I didn't doubt her integrity, but that I did doubt her credibility. I wanted to know if the "experts" she contacted really know anything about reading instruction, if they are acquainted with the latest research on other methods of instruction, how balanced instruction stacks up against other more systematic programs used for at risk children, and where parents could learn more about the efficacy of this method. But I didn't ask any of those questions. I sat down. I know who butters my bread, and I'm a single parent with a child with special needs. I need my job.

What options does this teacher have? She spoke up in a reasonable, careful way. She knows what's at stake for her as a teacher in this system—her job is likely to be on the line if she presses further. Perhaps she's done all she can, given the real-world aspects of her situation. But others of us aren't constrained by fear of losing our jobs or other disciplinary action. We could ask more questions of people like Dr. Lane and other school board members.

Advising policy makers isn't easy, especially when they don't seem to see how they're adding to the tragicomedy of public education. However, regardless of the level at which education policy is being made, we need to keep hammering away at the fact that effective instruction, which is by definition research-based, is what schools should be about. This includes instruction in social and self-care skills as well as academic skills. Anything that enhances instruction contributes to the central mission of the schools. We need to base the selection of programs and instructional methods on the best field-test data we can find using our best logical thinking to search out the most reliable data we can find. If a program or method hasn't been field-tested and found to be effective, then there's no reason to adopt it.[7]

Wasteful spending and money for schools

A lot of money in our school budgets is wasted on instruction that isn't effective, that's for sure. *But we and our policy makers also need to understand that cutting this wasteful spending won't address all the financial needs of education.* Here's a proposition as irrational as any I've discussed: we can avoid the problem of increasing the money we spend on our schools by cutting out the waste in the education budget. I repeat: this idea that spending for education can be kept the same or reduced simply by being smarter about spending the money we have is pure poppycock. Sorry to say it because I know it'll disappoint a lot of people who might agree with much of what they've read to this point, but part of the tragicomedy of public education is la-la thinking about schooling and money—the cockeyed notions that money makes no appreciable difference in the quality of schooling, that the biggest problem is wasteful spending, and on and on.

A very large portion of state and local tax revenues (and an especially large percentage of local taxes) goes to funding public education. And although some schools, particularly those in more affluent communities, are reasonably well-funded, many schools in poor communities are grotesquely underfunded. As a consequence, many of the kids who are poor get particularly poor schooling; their schools

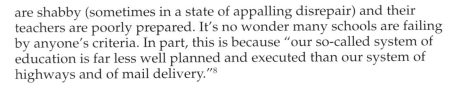

are shabby (sometimes in a state of appalling disrepair) and their teachers are poorly prepared. It's no wonder many schools are failing by anyone's criteria. In part, this is because "our so-called system of education is far less well planned and executed than our system of highways and of mail delivery."[8]

State and local funding and control of schools carry with them responsibilities for funding that are often poorly discharged, and the American emphasis on local control of schools also exacerbates inequities in education. Anti-tax sentiment is very strong at all levels of government. We want our children to understand that you usually get about what you pay for. But then we want excellence in their education on the cheap. Not smart.

In most of our schools, teachers are undervalued and underpaid. Many educators and many children understand that adults' talk about how much they value children isn't backed up by action—too many adults aren't willing to put their money where their mouth is. Too many adults don't want to pay taxes for schools their own children don't attend. Tragicomic, because these same adults will wonder why the products of our schools don't know more and don't provide them with good service. Duh!

Oh, well . . . I won't go on as much as I could about many adults' apparent belief in the "education fairy" (the educational equivalent of the tooth fairy) who somehow slips money into schools without anyone's being aware of it (lots of teachers end up spending their own money for things the public should but doesn't provide). Neither will I go further in describing the ridiculousness of the argument that if a school is doing a poor job we should just close it down or cut its budget (which makes about as much sense as abandoning your stalled car or hitting it with a sledge hammer).

Cut out wasteful spending on our schools? You bet. Provide more money for education, especially for poor kids, and make sure it's well spent? We must.

Let's do a better job of thinking and get after the policy makers, too

Mark Twain warned that we'll be tempted to go with the flow and embrace an opinion that's entitled to no respect at all because it represents little or no reflection.[9] We too often get suckered into ideas that would have been proven plainly untenable upon more careful

reflection. We let this happen because we play the sucker to others' artful use of strategies, as discussed in Part I of this book. Among the most seductive strategies, is that of stating something that's partly true—true enough to draw us into a larger falsehood, true enough to get us to ignore what's not true.

Perhaps the hard economic realities beginning in 2008 and the grand Ponzi scheme of Bernard Madoff have their counterparts in what we hear and read about education. Both the upbeat economic predictions of 2007 and the fraud of Bernie Madoff were based on partial truths, not on *total* fabrications. That's what made them so appealing to so many people—they could verify the partial truths and ignore what seemed inconvenient. And I fear that the truth about wasteful spending in education, which is only part of the story about funding our schools, will be used by many otherwise intelligent people to fool themselves and pull the wool over the eyes of others about the larger truth of the need for more money for most of our public schools, especially those in less affluent communities.

The funding issue, though, is just part of our poor thinking about education. Consider an editorial published on Christmas Day 2008 in the *Washington Post*.[10] The editorial suggests that the inevitability of achievement gaps is a myth that has been left behind, where it belongs. (Makes you think of leaving the "myth" of economic cycles behind.) After all, the editorial notes, an elementary school in a nearby county has achieved extraordinary success in raising the achievement of low-income ethnic minority students. The students in this school now compare favorably in achievement to others. This manifestly does *not* mean that every school can do the same. (Remember, *some* investors actually made money with Madoff, but Madoff's scheme was unsustainable and collapsed, leaving most with little or nothing.) And the newspaper editors quote the president of the Education Trust, saying that the performance of this school has shattered "the misguided and dangerous belief that achievement gaps are inevitable."

The whole truth is that some gaps aren't inevitable but some are. Large gaps in average achievement between low- and high-income students and between students varying in skin color or national origin are *not* inevitable just because of the homes they come from or economic circumstances or skin color. Yet, statistical gaps in average scores between high and low achievers, between schools, or school districts, or states, and so on *are* absolutely inevitable if we measure achievement. The reality of low achievers won't go away because we don't like it. The editorial and its quotation are partly true, but they ignore the inevitability of the kinds of gaps I've already discussed—gaps that the simple mathematics of statistics tell us will always be there if we measure achievement. No Child Left Behind Act doesn't acknowledge the fact that some gaps are inevitable. It assumes that all gaps are closable. One great tragicomic aspect of public education is that too few policy makers seem to be interested in thinking and talking about gaps that are inevitable and those that aren't.

Notes for Chapter Twelve

[1] Mark Twain (2008, p. 50)

[2] Gallagher (2007), Kowalski & Lasley (2009)

[3] See Kauffman & Konold (2007), Konold & Kauffman (2009)

[4] Gillon (2000); see also Kauffman (2009)

[5] See also Detrich, Keyworth, & States (2008)

[6] See Detrich et al. (2008), Hirsch (1996), Kauffman (2002), Ravitch (2000)

[7] Engelmann, Bateman, & Lloyd (2007), Hirsch (1996), Kauffman (2002)

[8] Shattuck (1999, p. 34)

[9] Mark Twain (2008)

[10] *Washington Post* (2008)

References and Websites

Bain, W. (1995). The loss of innocence: Lyotard, Foucault, and the challenge of postmodern education. In M. Peters (Ed.), *Education and the postmodern condition* (pp. 1–20). Westport, CT: Bergin & Garvey.

Baker, J. M., & Zigmond, N. (1995). The meaning and practice of inclusion for students with learning disabilities: Themes and implications from five cases. *The Journal of Special Education, 29*, 163–180.

Bateman, B. D. (2004). *Elements of successful teaching: A best practices handbook for beginning teachers.* Verona, WI: Attainment.

Bateman, B. D., & Linden, M. A. (2006). *Better IEPs: How to develop legally correct and educationally useful programs* (4th ed.). Verona, WI: Attainment.

Becker, W. C., & Gersten, R. (2001). Follow-up of Follow Through: The later effects of the direct instruction model on children in fifth and sixth grades. *Journal of Direct Instruction, 1*(1), 57–71.

Betebenner, D. W. (2008, March 20). Norm- and criterion-referenced student growth. Dover, NH: National Center for the Improvement of Educational Assessment.

Blackburn, S. (2005). *Truth: A guide.* New York: Oxford University Press.

Blount, R., Jr. (2001). Mark Twain's reconstruction. *Atlantic Monthly, 288*(1), 67–81.

Brock, W., Marshall, R., & Tucker, M. (2009, May 30). 10 steps to world-class schools. *Washington Post,* A19.

Carnine, D. (1993). The contributions of a scientific/business perspective to improving American education. *Effective School Practices, 12*(1), 63–65.

Carnine, D. (1998, June). *The metamorphosis of education into a mature profession.* Eugene, OR: National Center to Improve the Tools of Educators.

Carnine, D. (2000). *Why education experts resist effective practices (and what it would take to make education more like medicine).* Washington, DC: Fordham Foundation.

Carnine, D. W., Silbert, J., Kame'enui, E. J., & Tarver, S. G. (2005). *Teaching struggling and at-risk readers: A direct instruction approach.* Upper Saddle River, NJ: Merrill Prentice-Hall.

Carnine, D. W., Silbert, J., Kame'enui, E. J., & Tarver, S. G. (2010). *Direct instruction reading* (5th ed.). Upper Saddle River, NJ: Merrill Prentice-Hall.

Charlottesville Daily Progress. (2003, June 1). All-or-nothing tests causing states grief; Florida, Virginia among those considering changes. B1, B4.

Clemens, S. L. (1899, 1976). Christian Science and the book of Mrs. Eddy. In *Mark Twain: Collected tales, sketches, speeches, & essays, 1891-1910* (pp. 371–389). New York: Library of America.

Conquest, R. (2000). *Reflections on a ravaged century.* New York: Norton.

Cook, B. G., Gerber, M. M., & Semmel, M. I. (1997). Are effective school reforms effective for all students? The implications of joint outcome production for school reform. *Exceptionality, 7,* 77–95.

Crews, F. (2001). *Postmodern Pooh.* New York: North Point Press.

Dasenbrock, R. W. (1995). We've done it to ourselves: The critique of truth and the attack on theory. In J. Williams (Ed.), *PC Wars: Politics and theory in the academy* (pp. 172–183). New York: Routledge.

Day, A. G. (Ed.). (1966). *Mark Twain's Letters from Hawaii.* Honolulu, HI: University of Hawaii Press.

Deno, S. L. (1997). Whether thou goest . . . perspectives on progress monitoring. In J. W. Lloyd, E. J. Kameenui, & D. Chard (Eds.), *Issues in educating students with disabilities* (pp. 77–99). Mahwah, NJ: Lawrence Erlbaum Associates.

Detrich, R., Keyworth, R., & States, J. (Eds.). (2008). *Advances in evidence-based education. Vol. I. A roadmap to evidence-based education.* Oakland, CA: Wing Institute.

Dorn, C. (2007). *American education, democracy and the Second World War.* New York: Palgrave Macmillan.

Ehrlich, R. (2001, May 20). They all laughed at Galileo, too. *Washington Post,* B3.

Elkind, D. (1998). Behavioral disorders: A postmodern perspective. *Behavioral Disorders, 23*, 153–159.

Engelmann, S. (1969). *Preventing failure in the primary grades.* Chicago: SRA.

Engelmann, S. (1997), Grossen, B. (1993), and Zigmond, N. (2003, 2007, 2009)

Engelmann, S. (1997). Theory of mastery and acceleration. In J. W. Lloyd, E. J. Kameenui, & D. Chard (Eds.), *Issues in educating students with disabilities* (pp. 177–195). Mahwah, NJ: Lawrence Erlbaum Associates.

Engelmann, S., Bateman, B. D., & Lloyd, J. W. (2007). *Educational logic and illogic.* Eugene, OR: Association for Direct Instruction.

Engelmann, S., & Carnine, D. (1982). *Theory of instruction: Principles and applications.* New York: Irvington.

Erickson, F., & Gutierrez, K. (2002). Culture, rigor, and science in educational research. *Educational Researcher, 31*(8), 21–24.

Esquith, R. (2007). *Teach like your hair's on fire: The methods and madness inside room 56.* New York: Viking.

Feynman, R. P. (1985). *"Surely you're joking, Mr. Feynman!" Adventures of a curious character.* New York: Norton.

Feynman, R. P. (1998). *The meaning of it all: Thoughts of a citizen scientist.* Cambridge, MA: Helix Books.

Feynman, R. P. (1999). *The pleasure of finding things out.* Cambridge, MA: Helix Books.

Finn, C. E., Jr., Rotherham, A. J., & Hokanson, C., R. Jr. (Eds.). (2001). *Rethinking special education for a new century.* New York: Thomas B. Fordham Foundation.

Forness, S. R. (2001). Special education and related services: What have we learned from meta-analysis? *Exceptionality, 9*, 185–197.

Forness, S. R., Kavale, K. A., Blum, I. M., & Lloyd, J. W. (1997). What works in special education and related services: Using meta-analysis to guide practice. *Teaching Exceptional Children, 29*(6), 4–9.

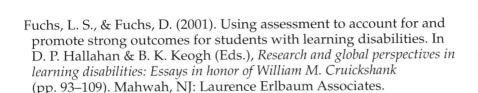

Fuchs, L. S., & Fuchs, D. (2001). Using assessment to account for and promote strong outcomes for students with learning disabilities. In D. P. Hallahan & B. K. Keogh (Eds.), *Research and global perspectives in learning disabilities: Essays in honor of William M. Cruickshank* (pp. 93–109). Mahwah, NJ: Laurence Erlbaum Associates.

Gadamer, H. G. (1959/1988). On the circle of understanding. In J. Connolly & T. Kleutner (Eds. & Trans.), *Hermeneutics versus science? Three German views: Essays by H. G. Gadamer, E. K. Specht, & W. Stagmuller* (pp. 68–78). Notre Dame, IN: University of Notre Dame Press.

Gallagher, D. J. (2004). Entering the conversation: The debate behind the debates in special education. In D. J. Gallagher (Ed.), *Challenging orthodoxy in special education: Dissenting voices* (pp. 3–26). Denver, CO: Love.

Gallagher, J. J. (1993). When ability grouping makes good sense. *Effective School Practices, 12*(1), 42–43.

Gallagher, J. J. (2007). *Driving change in special education.* Baltimore: Paul H. Brookes.

Gamoran, A. (1992). Is ability grouping equitable? *Educational Leadership, 50*(2), 11–17.

Gerber, M. M. (2005). Teachers are still the test: Limitations of response to instruction strategies for identifying children with learning disabilities. *Journal of Learning Disabilities, 38,* 516–524.

Gillon, S. M. (2000). *That's not what we meant to do: Reform and its unintended consequences in twentieth-century America.* New York: Norton.

Ginicola, M. M., & Saccoccio, C. (2008). Good intentions, unintended consequences: The impact of NCLB on children's mental health. *Emotional and Behavioral Disorders in Youth, 8*(2), 27–36.

Glod, M. (2009, May 16). Duncan delves behind grim statistics: Detroit students go face to face with education chief on what they need to succeed. *Washington Post,* A2.

Gould, S. J. (1996). *Full house: The spread of excellence from Plato to Darwin.* New York: Three Rivers Press.

Gould, S. J. (1997a). *Questioning the millennium. A rationalist's guide to a precisely arbitrary countdown.* New York: Harmony.

Gould, S. J. (1997b). The positive power of skepticism. Foreword in M. Shermer, *Why people believe weird things: Pseudoscience, superstition, and other confusions of our time.* New York: W. H. Freeman.

Gould, S. J. (2000). *The lying stones of Marrakech: Penultimate reflections on natural history.* New York: Three Rivers Press.

Grann, D. (2008, February 11 & 18). True crime: A postmodern murder mystery. *The New Yorker*, 120–135.

Gross, P. R. (1998). The Icarian impulse. *Wilson Quarterly, 22*, 39–49.

Gross, P. R., & Levitt, N. (1998). *Higher superstition: The academic left and its quarrels with science.* Baltimore: Johns Hopkins University Press.

Gross, P. R., Levitt, N., & Lewis, M. W. (Eds.). (1996). *The flight from science and reason.* Baltimore: Johns Hopkins University Press.

Grossen, B. (Ed.). (1993). Focus: Heterogeneous versus homogeneous grouping. *Effective School Practices, 12*(1).

Hahn, V. S. (2008, October 20). No school left behind: Even the best are failing; some of the highest-rated schools in the region are being tripped up by federal law. *St. Louis Post-Dispatch*, A1, A9.

Hallahan, D. P., Kauffman, J. M., & Pullen, P. C. (2009). *Exceptional learners: Introduction to special education* (11th ed.). Boston: Allyn & Bacon.

Harry, B., & Klingner, J. (2006). *Why are so many minority students in special education? Understanding race & disability in schools.* New York: Teachers College Press.

Harry, B., & Klingner, J. (2007). Discarding the deficit model. *Educational Leadership, 64*(5), 16–21.

Hecht, J. M. (2003). *Doubt: A history.* San Francisco: Harper.

Hesse, M. (2008, April 27). Can you handle it? Truth. Better yet: Do you know it when you see it? *Washington Post*, M1, M8.

Hirsch, E. D., Jr. (1987). *Cultural literacy: What every American needs to know.* New York: Houghton Mifflin.

Hirsch, E. D., Jr. (1996). *The schools we need and why we don't have them.* New York: Anchor.

Ho, A. D. (2008). The problem with "proficiency": Limitations of statistics and policy under No Child Left Behind. *Educational Researcher, 37,* 351–360.

Huefner, D. S. (2006). *Getting comfortable with special education law: A framework for working with children with disabilities* (2nd ed.). Norwood, MA: Christopher Gordon.

Jacobson, J. W., Mulick, J. A., & Foxx, R. M. (Eds.). (2005). *Controversial therapies for developmental disabilities: Fad, fashion, and science in professional practice.* Mahwah, NJ: Lawrence Erlbaum Associates.

Jarvis, E. (1852). On the supposed increase in insanity. *American Journal of Insanity, 8,* 333–364.

Johns, B. H. (2003). NCLB and IDEA: Never the twain should meet. *Learning Disabilities: A Multidisciplinary Journal, 12*(3), 89–91.

Kauffman, J. M. (1990, April). *What happens when special education works? The sociopolitical context of research in the 1990s.* Invited address, Special Education Special Interest Group, American Educational Research Association Meeting, Boston, MA.

Kauffman, J. M. (1999). The role of science in behavioral disorders. *Behavioral Disorders, 24,* 265–272.

Kauffman, J. M. (2002). *Education deform: Bright people sometimes say stupid things about education.* Lanham, MD: Rowman & Littlefield Education.

Kauffman, J. M. (2003a). Appearances, stigma, and prevention. *Remedial and Special Education, 24,* 195–198.

Kauffman, J. M. (2003b). Reflections on the field. *Behavioral Disorders, 28,* 205–208.

Kauffman, J. M. (2005). Waving to Ray Charles: Missing the meaning of disability. *Phi Delta Kappan, 86,* 520–521, 524.

Kauffman, J. M. (2008). Would we recognize progress if we saw it? A commentary. *Journal of Behavioral Education, 17,* 128–143.

Kauffman, J. M. (2009). Attributions of malice to special education policy and practice. In T. E. Scruggs & M. A. Mastropieri (Eds.), *Advances in learning and behavioral disabilities: Vol. 22. Policy and practice* (pp. 33–66). Bingley, UK: Emerald.

Kauffman, J. M., & Brigham, F. J. (2009). *Working with troubled children.* Verona, WI: Attainment.

Kauffman, J. M., Conroy, M., Gardner, R., & Oswald, D. (2008). Cultural sensitivity in the application of behavior principles to education. *Education and Treatment of Children, 31*, 239–262.

Kauffman, J. M., & Hallahan, D. P. (1997, 2005a). *Special education: What it is and why we need it.* Boston: Allyn & Bacon.

Kauffman, J. M., & Hallahan, D. P. (Eds.). (2005b). *The illusion of full inclusion: A comprehensive critique of a current special education bandwagon* (2nd ed.). Austin, TX: Pro-Ed.

Kauffman, J. M., & Hung, L. Y. (2009). Special education for intellectual disability: Current trends and perspectives. *Current Opinion in Psychiatry, 22*, 452–456.

Kauffman, J. M., & Konold, T. R. (2007). Making sense in education: Pretense (including NCLB) and realities in rhetoric and policy about schools and schooling. *Exceptionality, 15*, 75–96.

Kauffman, J. M., & Krouse, J. (1981). The cult of educability: Searching for the substance of things hoped for, the evidence of things not seen. *Analysis and Intervention in Developmental Disabilities, 1*, 53–60.

Kauffman, J. M., & Landrum, T. J. (2009a). *Characteristics of emotional and behavioral disorders of children and youth* (9th ed.). Upper Saddle River, NJ: Merrill Prentice-Hall.

Kauffman, J. M., & Landrum, T. J. (2009b). Politics, civil rights, and disproportional identification of students with emotional and behavioral disorders. *Exceptionality, 17*, 177–188.

Kauffman, J. M., Landrum, T. J., Mock, D. R., Sayeski, B., & Sayeski, K. L. (2005). Diverse knowledge and skills require a diversity of instructional groups: A position statement. *Remedial and Special Education, 26*, 2–6.

Kauffman, J. M., & Lloyd, J. W. (2009). Statistics, data, and special educational decisions. Manuscript submitted for publication,

University of Virginia.

Kauffman, J. M., McGee, K., & Brigham, M. (2004). Enabling or disabling? Observations on changes in the purposes and outcomes of special education. *Phi Delta Kappan, 85*, 613–620.

Kauffman, J. M., Mock, D. R., Mostert, M. P., & Kavale, K. A. (2008). The real-world consequences of the refusal of reason: The wrecking of teacher education. In M. P. Mostert, K. A. Kavale, & J. M. Kauffman (Eds.), *Challenging the refusal of reasoning in special education* (pp. 221–236). Denver, CO: Love.

Kauffman, J. M., Mock, D. R., & Simpson, R. L. (2007). Problems related to underservice of students with emotional or behavioral disorders. *Behavioral Disorders, 33*, 43–57.

Kauffman, J. M., Mock, D. R., Tankersley, M., & Landrum, T. J. (2008). Effective service delivery models. In R. J. Morris & N. Mather (Eds.), *Evidence-based interventions for students with learning and behavioral challenges* (pp. 359–378). Mahwah, NJ: Lawrence Erlbaum Associates.

Kauffman, J. M., Mostert, M. P., Trent, S. C., & Pullen, P. L. (2006). *Managing classroom behavior: A reflective case-based approach* (4th ed.). Boston: Allyn & Bacon.

Kauffman, J. M., & Pullen, P. L. (1996). Eight myths about special education. *Focus on Exceptional Children, 28*(5), 1–12.

Kauffman, J. M., & Sasso, G. M. (2006a). Toward ending cultural and cognitive relativism in special education. *Exceptionality, 14*, 65–90.

Kauffman, J. M., & Sasso, G. M. (2006b). Certainty, doubt, and the reduction of uncertainty: A rejoinder. *Exceptionality, 14*, 109–120.

Kazdin, A. E. (2008). *The Kazdin method for parenting the defiant child*. Boston: Houghton Mifflin.

King, C. I. (2001, December 15). Condoleezza Rice's oddball critic. *Washington Post*, A29.

Koertge, N. (Ed.). (1998). *A house built on sand: Exposing postmodernist myths about science*. New York: Oxford University Press.

Kohn, A. (2000). *The case against standardized testing: Raising the scores, ruining the schools*. Westport, CT: Heinemann.

Kohn, A. (2001). Fighting the tests: A practical guide to rescuing our schools. *Phi Delta Kappan, 82*, 349–357.

Konold, T. R., & Kauffman, J. M. (2009). The No Child Left Behind Act: Making decisions without data or other reality checks. In T. Kowalski & T. Lasley (Eds.), *Handbook of data-based decision making for education* (pp. 72–86). New York: Routledge.

Kowalski, T., & Lasley, T. (Eds.). (2009). *Handbook of data-based decision making for education*. New York: Routledge.

Krauthammer, C. (November 27, 2000). No more rule rewrites. *Washington Post*, A21.

Kundera, M. (1990). *Immortality* [translated by Peter Kussi]. New York: Grove Weidenfeld.

Landrum, T. J., & Kauffman, J. M. (2006). Behavioral approaches to classroom management. In C. M. Evertson & C. S. Weinstein (Eds.), *Handbook of classroom management: Research, practice, and contemporary issues* (pp. 47–71). Mahwah, NJ: Lawrence Erlbaum Associates.

Lemann, N. (2001, July 2). Testing limits: Can the President's education crusade survive Beltway politics? *The New Yorker*, 28–34.

Lewis, T. J., Newcomer, L. L., Trussell, R., & Richter, M. (2006). Schoolwide positive behavior support: Building systems to develop and maintain appropriate social behavior. In C. Evertson & C. Weinstein (Eds.), *Handbook of classroom management: Research, practice, and contemporary issues* (pp. 833–854). Mahwah, NJ: Lawrence Erlbaum Associates.

Lipsky, D. K, & Gartner, A. (1996). Inclusion, school restructuring, and the remaking of American society. *Harvard Educational Review, 66*, 762–796.

Lloyd, J. W., Forness, S. R., & Kavale, K. A. (1998). Some methods are more effective. *Intervention in School and Clinic, 33*(1), 195–200.

Lloyd, J. W., & Hallahan, D. P. (2007). Advocacy and reform of special education. In J. B. Crockett, M. M. Gerber, & T. J. Landrum (Eds.), *Achieving the radical reform of special education: Essays in honor of James M. Kauffman* (pp. 245–263). Mahwah, NJ: Lawrence Erlbaum Associates.

Loh, S. T. (2008). *Mother on fire: A true mother%#$@ story about parenting*. New York: Crown.

MacMillan, D. L., Gresham, F. M., & Forness, S. R. (1996). Full inclusion: An empirical perspective. *Behavioral Disorders, 21*, 145–159.

Marchand-Martella, N. E., Slocum, T. A., & Martella, R. C. (Eds.). (2004). *Introduction to Direct Instruction*. Boston: Allyn & Bacon.

Mark Twain. (2008, December 22 & 29). The privilege of the grave. *The New Yorker*, 50–51.

Mark Twain Foundation. (1967). *Mark Twain: Collected tales, sketches, speeches, & essays, 1852–1890*. New York: Library of America.

Mark Twain Foundation. (1976). *Mark Twain: Collected tales, sketches, speeches, & essays, 1891–1910*. New York: Library of America.

Mathews, J. (2003, November 11). No Child Left Behind Act: Facts and fiction. *Washington Post*, A8.

Mathews, J. (2008, April 13). The wrong yardstick. *Washington Post Magazine*, 22–23, 35.

Mock, D., & Kauffman, J. M. (2002). Preparing teachers for full inclusion: Is it possible? *Teacher Educator, 37*, 202–215.

Mock, D. R., & Kauffman, J. M. (2005). The delusion of full inclusion. In J. W. Jacobson, J. A. Mulick, & R. M. Foxx (Eds.), *Fads: Dubious and improbable treatments for developmental disabilities* (pp. 113–128). Mahwah, NJ: Lawrence Erlbaum Associates.

Morris, R. M., & Mather, N. (Eds.) (2008). *Evidence-based interventions for students with learning and behavioral challenges*. Mahwah, NJ: Lawrence Erlbaum Associates.

Mostert, M. P., Kavale, K. A., & Kauffman, J. M. (Eds.). (2008). *Challenging the refusal of reasoning in special education*. Denver, CO: Love.

Mungazi, D. A. (1999). *The evolution of educational theory in the United States*. Westport, CT: Praeger.

National Center on Education and the Economy. (1989). *To secure our future*. Rochester, NY: Author.

Neider, C. (Ed.). (1917/1966). *The autobiography of Mark Twain*. New York: Harper & Row Perennial Library.

Neiman, S. (2008). *Moral clarity: A guide for grown-up idealists*. New York: Harcourt.

Oliphant, T. (2001, June 17). Actually, not just rhetorically, leaving no child behind. *Boston Globe*, C2.

Orwell, G. (1954, original essay 1946). Politics and the English language. In *A collection of essays by George Orwell* (pp. 162–177). New York: Doubleday Anchor.

Pillow, W. S. (2000). Deciphering attempts to decipher postmodern educational research. *Educational Researcher, 29*(5), 21–24.

Pulliam, J. D., & Van Patten, J. J. (2003). *History of education in America* (8th ed.). Upper Saddle River, NJ: Prentice Hall.

Raspberry, W. (2001, February 5). No-excuses education. *Washington Post*, A19.

Ravitch, D. (2000). *Left back: A century of failed school reforms*. New York: Simon & Schuster.

Rhodes, W. C. (1987). Ecology and the new physics. *Behavioral Disorders, 13*, 58–61.

Rosenshine, B. (1997). Advances in research on instruction. In J. W. Lloyd, E. J. Kameenui, & D. Chard (Eds.), *Issues in educating students with disabilities* (pp. 197–220). Mahwah, NJ: Lawrence Erlbaum Associates.

Rosenshine, B. (2008). Systematic instruction. In T. L. Good (Ed.), *21st Century education: A reference handbook: Vol. 1* (pp. 235–243). Thousand Oaks, CA: Sage.

Rothman, E. P., & Berkowitz, P. H. (1967). The clinical school—A paradigm. In P. H. Berkowitz & E. P. Rothman (Eds.), *Public education for disturbed children in New York City* (pp. 355–369). Springfield, IL: Thomas.

Rothstein, R., Jacobsen, R., & Wilder, T. (2006, November). *"Proficiency for all"—An oxymoron*. Paper presented at a symposium on "Examining America's commitment to closing achievement gaps: NCLB and its alternatives." New York: Teachers College, Columbia University.

Ryan, K., & Cooper, J. M. (Eds.). (2004). *Kaleidoscope: Readings in education* (10th ed.). Boston: Houghton Mifflin.

Ryan, S., & Grieshaber, S. (2005). Shifting the developmental to postmodern practices in early childhood teacher education. *Journal of Teacher Education, 56*, 34–45.

Sarason, S. B. (1990). *The predictable failure of school reform: Can we change course before it's too late?* San Francisco: Jossey-Bass.

Sasso, G. M. (2001). The retreat from inquiry and knowledge in special education. *Journal of Special Education, 34*, 178–193.

Sasso, G. M. (2007). Science and reason in special education: The legacy of Derrida and Foucault. In J. B. Crockett, M. M. Gerber, & T. J. Landrum (Eds.), *Achieving the radical reform of special education: Essays in honor of James M. Kauffman* (pp. 143–167). Mahwah, NJ: Lawrence Erlbaum Associates.

Shattuck, R. (1999). *Candor & perversion: Literature, education, and the arts*. New York: Norton.

Shavelson, R. J., & Towne, L. (Eds.). (2002). *Scientific research in education*. Washington, DC: National Academies Press.

Shermer, M. (1997). *Why people believe weird things: Pseudoscience, superstition, and other confusions of our time*. New York: W. H. Freeman.

Shermer, M. (2001). *The borderlands of science: Where sense meets nonsense*. New York: Oxford University Press.

Skiba, R. J., & Rausch, M. K. (2006). Zero tolerance, suspension, and expulsion: Questions of equity and effectiveness. In C. M. Evertson & C. S. Weinstein (Eds.), *Handbook of classroom management: Research, practice, and contemporary issues* (pp. 1063–1089). Mahwah, NJ: Lawrence Erlbaum Associates.

Slevin, P. (2000, December 30). The name on Bush's signature issue. *Washington Post*, A6, A8.

Sokal, A., & Bricmont, J. (1998). *Fashionable nonsense: Postmodern intellectuals' abuse of science*. New York: Picador.

Specter, M. (2007, March 12). Annals of science. The denialists: The dangerous attacks on the consensus about H.I.V. and AIDS. *The New Yorker*, 32–38.

St. Pierre, E. A. (2000). The call for intelligibility in postmodern educational research. *Educational Researcher, 29*(5), 25–28.

Stribling, F. T. (1842). Physician and superintendent's report. In *Annual Reports to the Court of Directors of the Western Lunatic Asylum to the Legislature of Virginia* (pp. 1–70). Richmond, VA: Shepherd & Conlin.

Tanner, D. (2000). Manufacturing problems and selling solutions: How to succeed in the education business without really educating. *Phi Delta Kappan, 82*, 188–202.

Tashman, B. (1996). Our failure to follow through. *Effective School Practices, 15*(1), 67.

Tolson, J. (1998). At issue: The many and the one. *Wilson Quarterly, 22*, 12.

Tong, S. (2006, September 27). Straight talk equals good business. *Marketplace*.

Towne, L., Wise, L. L., & Winters, T. M. (Eds.). (2004). *Advancing scientific research in education*. Washington, DC: National Academies Press.

Twain, M. (1894/1969). *Pudd'nhead Wilson*. New York: Penguin.

Twain, M., & Warner, C. D. (1874/2008). *The gilded age*. Toledo, OH: American Publishing Company/San Diego: ICON Classics.

Usher, R., & Edwards, R. (1994). *Postmodernism and education: Different voices, different words*. London: Routledge.

Vaughn, S., Hughes, M. T., Moody, S. W., & Elbaum, B. (2001). Instructional grouping for reading for students with LD: Implications for practice. *Intervention in School and Clinic, 36*, 131–137.

Wagoner, J. L., Jr. (2004). *Jefferson and education*. Charlottesville, VA: Thomas Jefferson Foundation.